THE
HEART OF
ENGLAND
WAY

RECREATIONAL PATH GUIDE

THE
HEART OF
ENGLAND
WAY

RICHARD SALE

Photographs by the Author

Aurum Press

Ordnance
Survey

Richard Sale is a physicist by training; but after many years of attempting to prevent the frontiers of science from falling on him, he gave up the struggle and became a writer/photographer. He specializes in books on outdoor themes and has written many walking guides. He lives in the Cotswolds, just a short distance from the Heart of England Way.

First published in 1998 by Aurum Press Limited, 25 Bedford Avenue, London WC1B 3AT in association with the Ordnance Survey.

A catalogue record for this book is available from the British Library.

ISBN 1 85410 538 8

Book designed by Robert Updegraff
Printed and bound in Italy by Printers Trento Srl

Front Cover: *The Way at the edge of Bannam's Wood*
Title page: *Looking north from above Milford Common*

CONTENTS

The Heart of England Way

Circular walks will be found on pages: 54, 86 and 88

How to use this Guide

This guide is in three parts:

• The introduction, historical background to the area and advice for walkers.

• The path itself, described in seven chapters, with maps opposite each route description. This part of the guide also includes information on places of interest as well as a number of related short circular walks. Key sites are numbered in the text and on the maps to make it easy to follow the route description.

• The last part includes useful information such as local transport, accommodation, organizations involved with the path, and further reading.

The maps have been prepared by the Ordnance Survey® for this guide using 1 : 25 000 Pathfinder® and Explorer™ maps as a base. The line of the Heart of England Way is shown in yellow, with the status of each section of the path – footpath or bridleway for example – shown in green underneath (see key on inside front cover). These rights of way markings also indicate the precise alignment of the path at the time of the original surveys, but in some cases the yellow line on these maps may show a route which is different from that shown by those older surveys, and in such cases walkers are recommended to follow the yellow route in this guide. Any parts of the path that may be difficult to follow on the ground are clearly highlighted in the route description, and important points to watch for are marked with letters in each chapter, both in the text and on the maps. *Some maps start on a right-hand page and continue on the left-hand page – black arrows (➜) at the edge of the maps indicate the start point.* Should there have been a need to alter the route since publication of this guide for any reason, walkers are advised to follow the waymarks or signs which have been put up on site to indicate this.

Distance Checklist

This list will assist you in calculating distances between places on the Heart of England Way, planning overnight stops, checking your progress or planning links to other paths. The distances are between places on the Way and do not include diversions to places off the route. At many locations neither accomodation nor refreshment is available and you are advised to obtain an accommodation list. If you are planning your route using the Landranger® (1: 50 000) maps you will be able to identify all the locations below.

Location	Approximate distance from previous location	
	miles	*km*
Bourton-on-the-Water	0	0
Longborough	8	12.8
Blockley	5	8.0
Chipping Campden	3	4.8
Quinton	7	11.2
Bidford-on-Avon	7	11.2
Alcester	5	4.8
Henley-in-Arden	8	5.0
Baddesley Clinton Manor	6	9.6
Balsall Common	5	8.0
Berkswell	3	4.8
Meriden	2.5	4.0
Shustoke	6.5	10.4
Kingsbury Water Park (Broomey Croft Car Park)	1.5	2.4
Drayton Bassett	3	4.8
Lichfield (Horse & Jockey)	7.5	12.0
Lichfield (Cathedral)	2	3.2
Creswell Green	3	4.8
Castle Ring	3	4.8
Cannock Chase Visitor Centre	4	6.4
Milford Common	5	8.0

INTRODUCTION

Where the route skirts fields planted with wheat, poppies are a familiar sight. This field is near Nether Whitacre, north of the Shustoke Reservoirs.

Shakespeare country and the Cotswolds – there could hardly be a better definition of Englishness. Add to that the village with a justifiable claim to being the very centre of England and you have the ingredients which fully justify the name Heart of England.

The Heart of England Way heads northwards from Bourton-on-the-Water, one of the Cotswolds' main tourist centres, crossing the Avon Valley (at the eastern end of the Vale of Evesham) to reach the Forest of Arden. In Shakespeare's time the forest covered a great expanse of country to the west of Stratford-upon-Avon. Much has been cleared, felled to make charcoal, but enough remains to stir memories of scenes in some of the poet's best-loved plays.

North again, the Way enters the Tame Valley, a wide, flat and fertile valley which is crossed to reach Lichfield, one of the prettiest and most unspoilt cities of Middle England. Turning west the Way climbs to Cannock Chase, the most spectacular natural landscape in the Midlands, crossing the high, heathland plateau to finish at Milford on the Staffordshire and Worcestershire Canal.

On its journey the Way forges a route through one of the most densely populated areas of Britain. It crosses canals, the arteries that kept the Black Country's industrial heart beating by supplying raw materials, and exported its products. It crosses motorways, the arteries of the modern era, the noise of traffic occasionally acting as a beacon to the wayfarer. Equally noisy, but less useful as a waymarker, are the aircraft from Birmingham's airport. These noises might seem intrusions, and there are few walkers who would willingly trade quiet peace for a motorway bridge. But they are minor intrusions that merely remind walkers of where they are. In the main the Way crosses pastoral scenery as fine as any in England. True there is a continuous reminder of man's involvement in the landscape – but that merely aids an exploration of English development in the Heart of England.

WALKING THE WAY

The route is described from south to north simply because the prevailing weather in England tends to be from the south-west and so will be at the walker's back. In reality that is of minor concern: the Heart of England Way is essentially a lowland route, with no part rising above the 800 foot contour (above about 250 m). It is, therefore, never weather-swept in the way that exposed mountain ridges are. But the rain is still as wet and winds still as cold, and sensible clothing should be worn or carried against the possibility of a storm. Apart from Cannock Chase, with its forest tracks, and stretches of road or canal towpath, the Way crosses farmland. Its gradients are gentle, its climbs short, as much of the ground covered is gently undulating (when it is not actually flat). Boots that might also see service on a mountain crag are not, then, essential, though, as always, it is sensible to wear a shoe or lightweight boot that will allow the miles to be covered in comfort.

The Way follows the eastern edge of the Vale of Evesham, crossing the River Avon at Bidford, just beyond the picturesque weir at Barton.

The Cotswolds were once famous for their woollen cloth, the area's fast flowing streams driving the wool mills. This one is at Lower Slaughter.

The clearing, the erection of stiles and the waymarking of the Heart of England Way has largely been the result of the work of enthusiasts rather than official bodies, and it is a huge tribute to those volunteers that the waymarking is as good as it is, the Way's symbol (a green tree on a white disc) being seen regular and at virtually all key points. There are also a dozen bronze waymarkers set in the pavements to help Wayfarers through Lichfield. Nevertheless, the waymarking is not complete in a few places, and in others 'humorists' have removed, damaged, or even altered the position of the waymarkers. The instructions given in the book are therefore occasionally more detailed than the walker would find necessary if the waymarking was perfect.

The guide is divided into seven chapters, each corresponding to a reasonable day's walking (about 14½ miles / 23km) if a little time is allowed for exploration of the interesting sites along the way. Fortuitously, the chapter/day ends fall at towns where accommodation and transport is easily obtained.

THE COTSWOLDS

The Cotswolds are not true hills, despite the occasional use of the word. The appearance of hills comes from the carving of deep river valleys in an otherwise flat, but raised, plateau of oolitic limestone – a hard, impermeable rock named (from the Greek *oion lithos*, egg stone) for its granular structure, like fish roe. The plateau, its limestone laid down beneath a clear sea, was raised by gigantic earth movements. But it was not raised cleanly, being tilted east-west to form a characteristic scarp slope/dip slope geometry. To the west, the scarp, the Cotswold edge, forms a continuous wall – almost 100 miles (160 km) long and followed by the Cotswold Way – when viewed from across the Severn. To the east, the Cotswolds' plateau descends gently into Oxfordshire.

The Cotswolds have been important since man first left a permanent mark on the landscape. Neolithic (New Stone Age) man farmed the high uplands – the 'wolds' of the name – letting his pigs feed on the beechmast of the area's forests. He buried his dead (the important ones at least) in long barrows, large chambers constructed of stone slabs earthed over to form the mound that gives the tomb its common name. So distinctive were the barrows of the area that they are termed the Severn-Cotswold type to distinguish them from other forms.

When the Iron Age folk came, they, too, settled in the area, finding the Cotswolds' scarp edge and occasional isolated hillocks perfect for their hill forts. One such hill topped by a fort, Meon Hill, is passed along the Way.

The Romans settled in the Cotswolds soon after their invasion of 43AD, building roads across the high limestone plateau – Fosse Way, Akeman Street, Ryknild Street – and setting up the fortress town of *Corinium* (Cirencester) from which to launch their westward push against the Celts. The main Roman remains of the northern Cotswolds – the Chedworth Villa and *Corinium* itself – lie south of the Way, but one feature of Roman Cotswolds was to have a profound effect on the later history of the area. Many experts believe that it was the Romans who introduced the sheep that was to become the Cotswold Lion, the source not only of Cotswold, but of English wealth during the Middle Ages. The sheep, reared on the wolds, produced a thick fleece, one that weighted 28lbs (12.7 kilos, or two stones if weighed against the standard 'stones' carried by the wool merchants). So good was Cotswold wool that merchants travelled vast distances to buy it. Francesco di Marco Datini, the Tuscan buyer famed as the *Merchant of Prato*, came here, a journey that would tire today's car-borne traveller and which, with poor roads and the possibility of highwaymen, must have been truly daunting.

Soon the wool trade dominated the English economy and the Cotswolds produced more than half the cloth. Every other worker in the area was involved in the industry in some way and over 500,000 sheep roamed the high wolds. So important were the shepherds that they received a bowl of whey daily in summer, ewes' milk on Sundays, a lamb at weaning, and a fleece at shearing.

The Cotswold wool merchants became rich almost beyond imagining, so rich that kings and the exchequer borrowed from them. Despite their wealth most of the merchants did not lose sight of the source of their wealth: one merchant had this verse inscribed on his house -

I praise God and ever shall
It is the sheep hath paid for it all

After the collapse of the Cotswold woollen trade the 'Cotswold Lion' almost became extinct, but is now being bred again at several places in the area.

The rich Cotswold wool merchants raised the famous 'Wool Churches'. One of the finest, St James at Chipping Campden, is passed along the Way.

Because of this understanding the merchants did not, with rare exceptions, build extravagant houses, preferring to endow churches of great beauty. One of the finest of these wool churches is at Chipping Campden, and is passed along the Way.

Eventually the wool trade declined. Desperately, the government sought to prevent this decline, even to the extent of passing the Burial in Woollen Act which declared that 'from and after 1st August 1678 ... no corps of any person ... to be buried in any stuffe or things other than what is made of sheep's wool only'. But even this failed to halt the trade's demise.

When the wool trade collapsed the effect on the Cotswolds was devastating, with whole villages of folk starving or moving from the area. It is ironical that the stagnation this brought to the area, with development of many towns and villages ceasing several centuries ago, has led to the Cotswolds becoming one of Britain's foremost tourist area. In villages such as Lower Slaughter, Bourton-on-the-Hill, Blockley and Chipping Campden, all visited along the Way, the beautiful, warm-stoned cottages stand now as they have for centuries, time-capsuled by the end of an era and a way of life. Today the Cotswold Lion can only be found in farms specializing in rare breeds, though more common sheep breeds will occasionally be seen by the wayfarer. There will be cattle, too, and, as the walker descends from the high wolds, fields of cereals and the bright yellow, oily-perfumed rape.

With its stone-built cottages, Blockley is the ideal Cotswold village.

Though occasionally over-run with tourists at the height of summer, Bourton-on-the

... vater remains one of the area's loveliest villages.

THE VALE OF EVESHAM

Just a mile north of Chipping Campden is Dover's Hill, first landmark on the Cotswold Way and the scene of Robert Dover's Olympick Games, begun in the early seventeenth century and featuring such favourite sports as singlestick fighting, where the object was to break your opponent's head with your stick (and to prevent him doing the same to you) and shin kicking, which needs no explanation. The Games were stopped in about 1850 after the labourers building the railway line below the Cotswold Edge (and crossed along the Way) had succeeded in turning it into a drunken brawl that threatened the tranquillity of Chipping Campden's folk. More recently Dover's Olympick Games have been revived, though the International Olympic Committee has, perhaps unsurprisingly, so far failed to make the main events official Olympic sports.

At Dover's Hill the Cotswold Edge has turned sharply east so that the walkers on the scarp top are looking not west across the Edge (as they would have done on any of the 100 miles to the south), but north. And northwards, their gaze is across the Vale of Evesham, the broad, flat valley of the River Avon. The Vale, set on blue liassic limestone and topped by glacial moraine, is one of Britain's most fertile area, a centre for fruit growing and market gardening which is especially well known for the asparagus it produces.

Evesham, the town for which the Vale is named, was the site of one of England's great abbeys, founded for Benedictine monks by Bishop Egwin of Worcester in 714. The town that grew up around the abbey was an important place in medieval times, even more so after a bridge was built across the Avon. At the town, on 4 August 1265, the army of Prince Edward, son of Henry III, met that of Simon de Montfort.

When King John died in 1216, just a year after signing the Magna Carta, he was succeeded by his nine-year-old son, Henry III. In the early years of his reign, while power was held by regents, England was a reasonably peaceful and ordered place, but Henry grew into an incompetent king, his failed French adventures resulting in high taxes which, together with his flouting of the provisions of the Magna Carta, fuelled renewed hostility among the nobility. Simon de Montfort emerged as the nobles' leader, an odd choice in what was seen as a conflict between English nobles and a French king, as Simon was French by birth, and was also Henry's brother-in-law, being married to Eleanor, the king's sister.

In 1258 Simon compelled the king to accept a series of demands that went far beyond the provisions of the Magna Carta. The demands, which included the setting up of a council to draft a constitution limiting royal powers, were seen as usurping the king's powers and civil war followed. In a decisive battle near Lewes, Sussex, in May 1264, Simon emerged the victor, imprisoning Henry and his son, Prince Edward, and summoning a Great Council to which all shires and major towns sent two representatives. This is rightly viewed as the start of parliamentary democracy in England, with Simon seen as its champion.

But Prince Edward, who was being held captive in Hereford, escaped and raised an army. There were skirmishes around Hereford with Simon's army, then Edward marched towards Kenilworth, Simon's castle and the seat of his power. There, an inconclusive battle resulted in the capture of some of Simon's banners. Simon, hearing of Edward's attack, immediately marched towards Kenilworth, but was intercepted by Edward at Evesham and during a thunderstorm the decisive battle of the 'Baron's War' was fought.

Some historians believe that Edward's subterfuge with Simon's captured banners led Simon's army into an ambush, others that Edward's cunning use of a hidden ravine caused Simon's army to be trapped. Either way Edward circled Simon's army and annihilated it. Simon's mutilated corpse was taken to Evesham Abbey where it was buried before the high altar. Following the battle Edward's army marched again on Kenilworth, capturing it after a long and bloody siege.

The Heart of England Way does not visit Evesham, but somewhere it crosses the route taken by Edward's army at it moved between the town and Kenilworth Castle. Simon de Montfort's House of Commons may have been short-lived, but it was reconvened by Edward (by then King Edward I) within ten years of the battle. Thoughts of the basis of our democratic systems being fought over just a few kilometres away add an extra dimension to the crossing of the Vale of Evesham. If you are walking this part of the Way during the early morning, with a soft mist clinging to the flat land, you could almost imagine yourself stumbling across a colourful medieval army, its soldiers with their supply wagons and camp followers grumbling their way towards battle.

Being confined to Warwickshire, the Way explores the eastern edge of the Vale of Evesham, the most famous part of the Vale lying across the border in Worcestershire. Along the Way there are no orchards, the fertile fields growing cereals and vegetables, the latter mostly broad beans at the time of writing, the elegant tall plants and pretty flowers making a change from the acres of wheat.

The Vale of Evesham is drained by Shakepeare's Avon. The Way crosses the river a

Bidford-on-Avon.

THE FOREST OF ARDEN

'Are not these woods more free from peril than the envious court?' asks the banished Duke in Shakespeare's *As You Like It*, comparing the tranquillity of the Forest of Arden to the dangers of his usurped court.

But when, later in the play, Rosalind, Celia and Touchstone are in the Forest, Touchstone, in reply to Rosalind, states, 'Ay, now I am in Arden; the more fool I; when I was at home, I was in a better place: but travellers must be content.'

The quotes, of course, have to be seen in the context of the play, but they do highlight one of strange paradoxes of medieval (and earlier) forests. On the one hand, they supplied many of the necessities of life – wood for fuel, building and tools; food for domestic pigs; a place for hunting and for peace and quiet away from the rigours of village life. Yet they were also a place of foreboding. Travellers could be lost in the forest, fall prey to wild animals or bands of outlaws or, worse, to evil spirits and other supernatural creatures that most folk believed lurked in the densest thickets. To help travellers lost in the wood a light burned each night in the tower of Astley church, and a most welcome beacon it must have been as shadows lengthened and the imaginations of superstitious minds grew in sympathy.

The Midlands Plain is a fertile landscape, its fertility created by glaciers pushing south-east from Snowdonia and south-westwards from eastern England, which heaped fine-tilled moraine on to the land. The Forest of Arden grew in that fertile soil. Arden is Saxon, meaning woodland, the Saxons distinguishing this area of Warwickshire from that to the east (closer to Stratford) which they called Feldon (meaning more open country). But the Forest of Arden was not a continuous forest: William Camden, the Elizabethan traveller, noted that the area was 'for the most part thick set with woods, yet not without pastures, cornfields and sundry mines of iron'. The forested areas seem to have been many and large, and perhaps were once continuous, but clearing for agriculture, felling for timber – the half-timbered houses in Shakespeare's Stratford would have been built with wood from Arden trees – and, later, burning for charcoal to fuel iron furnaces, led to a reduction of the forest. Charcoal production, the use of bark in the leather tanning industry and country crafts such as furniture making (including the delightfully named bodgers, who turned the chair legs) led to a gradual decline in the forest, but with the Industrial Revolution the demand for charcoal rose and the destruction of Arden gathered pace. Only the development of coke-burning furnaces saved the forest

Near Mickleton are two of England's finest gardens. Here at Hidcote Manor the National Trust now maintains the garden created by Lawrence Johnston.

The second garden close to Mickleton, at Kiftsgate Court, is famous for growing the largest rose in England.

from total annihilation, though what remained was severely depleted by Dutch Elm disease which eliminated the remaining elm trees, once so numerous they were known as Warwickshire weeds.

The fertility of the Midlands Plain, the Feldon and the cleared Arden Forest, led to economic prosperity and that, in turn, to political importance. The area has often been called the 'Cockpit of England' because of battles critical to English history fought there. The first and last battles of the Civil War were fought on the Plain, at Edgehill and Naseby. And – arguably the most critical of all – at

Bosworth Field where Richard III's crown was retrieved from a thorn-bush and placed on the head of Henry Tudor, ushering in the most distinctive of all English royal dynasties.

Though the crown was the greatest prize won by Henry Tudor at Bosworth Field, there were other trophies, one of which was Warwick Castle. Though it lies a few miles to the east, few who walk the Heart of England Way will be able to resist a visit to what many consider to be the finest castle in England. The castle was a fitting trophy for Henry Tudor: Bosworth Field was the last battle of the Wars of the Roses, and the Wars' greatest player had been Richard Neville, Earl of Warwick. Neville at one time held both the Lancastrian King, Henry VI (whom he had defeated at the battle of St Albans in 1455) and the Yorkist King, Edward IV, captive. Finally in 1471, at Barnet, Neville was killed when his army was routed by that of Edward IV. In *Henry IV, Part 3*, Shakespeare has Edward, Earl of March (later Edward IV) calling Neville 'Thou setter up and plucker down of Kings', and Neville has been called 'Warwick the Kingmaker' since that time.

The Shakespearean quote is no surprise: the history and, indeed, the geography of Arden seems tied to that of William Shakespeare. The cottage of Mary Arden, William's mother, lies a short distance to the east of Alcester and the Way, while the main Shakespearean properties – Anne Hathaway's Cottage and the Stratford houses – lie only a little further away. Although Shakespeare was a Stratford man, along this section of the Way walkers are as close as it is now possible to be to the English countryside that inspired the poet. As way-farers follow the eastern edge of Bannam's Wood, approaching Henley-in-Arden, the view to their right (south-eastwards) is across a Feldon landscape that the poet might still recognize, while to the left is the wood itself, a remnant of an ancient Arden. In its wildest parts, some seen along the Way, it is still the country described by Shakespeare in *A Midsummer Night's Dream*. Though Act II, Scene 1 is supposed to be set in a wood near Athens, it is clearly Arden that inspired the words spoken by Oberon:

> I know a bank where the wild thyme blows,
> Where oxlips and the nodding violet grows,
> Quite over-canopied with luscious woodbine,
> With sweet musk-roses and with eglantine

Eglantine 1s the old word for sweet briar, and it can still be seen along the Way, as can the other plants mentioned, though with the decline of woodland areas they are now mostly seen in the hedgerows that separate the cereal and dairy herd fields.

Though the smallest cathedral in England, Lichfield, with its soaring nave and many art treasures, is also one of the finest.

LICHFIELD

'I lately took my friend Boswell and showed him genuine civilised life in an English provincial town. I turned him loose in Lichfield, my native city, that he might see for once real civility.'

It seems a strange decision to offer a city as a highlight of a long-distance footpath – surely the point of such paths is to escape urban rigours? But as this quotation from Samuel Johnson, the city's most famous son, makes clear, Lichfield is no ordinary city. Here, at the heart of the English Midlands, an area synonymous with industrialization and urban development, is a wonderfully genteel city: an architectural gem of a place, of manageable size and surrounded by delightful country.

To the south of the city, where Ryknild Street and Watling Street crossed, the Romans built *Letocetum* – Wall Village – at first just a fortress, but later expanding into what could perhaps best be described as a 'chariot stop'. But here, as elsewhere, when the Saxons came a century or so after the Romans had departed, they chose to settle away from the ruins of *Letocetum*. Saxon Lichfield was part of the Kingdom of Mercia, a kingdom which, in the early seventh century, was largely pagan, despite having a Christian bishop at Repton. In 669 a new bishop was appointed. Chad had been a student of the great St Aidan at Lindisfarne and was already renowned as a scholarly and good man. Chad moved the seat of his see from Repton to Lichfield and set about the task of converting the Mercians. He was highly successful, so much so that on his death his tomb became a place of pilgrimage for Saxons drawn by his godly reputation. When miracles started to occur at the tomb, the number of pilgrims increased and in the year 700 a cathedral was raised around a shrine containing the remains of the now-sanctified bishop. The Normans replaced the Saxon cathedral in the late eleventh century, the present building dating from the twelfth century.

The cathedral, Britain's smallest, took 150 years to complete, a time span which covered several changes of style in church architecture, though it takes an expert to identify these. The layman sees a Gothic church in red sandstone, its west front a forest of statuary, its three spires – known as the Ladies of the Vale – dominating the town. Inside, the cathedral is a masterpiece of height and elegance, the view along the nave being one of the most inspiring along the Way.

Henry VIII's Reformation saw an end to pilgrimages, and St Chad's shrine was torn down, his relics destroyed. Today a memorial tablet in the floor in front of the Lady Chapel marks the original position of the shrine. But though the shrine is gone there is still much to see: the Lady Chapel with its magnificent sixteenth-century stained glass, brought here in 1803 when the Herkenrode convent in Belgium was suppressed; *The Sleeping Children*, the moving memorial to two young sisters who died in 1812; and, best of all, the Lichfield Gospels, early eighth-century decorated Latin texts which have been at the cathedral for a thousand years.

Outside the cathedral, the Cathedral Close is the most complete in England, an array of superb houses dating from the fifteenth through to the seventeenth centuries. On the Close's northern edge are the Deanery and Old Bishop's Palace: at the north-western corner an arch leads to the black and white cottages of Vicar's Close where the cathedral's professional choristers once lived.

To the south of the cathedral is Minster Pool, its shape an echo of the Serpentine in Hyde Park thanks to the insistence of the poet Anna Steward, the daughter of a cathedral canon. The view of the cathedral from across the pool (particularly from its western edge) is arguably the finest in the town. South again, along Dam Street, followed by the Way, is Market Square. Here stand statues of Dr Samuel Johnson and his friend and biographer James Boswell. Johnson was born in the house on the corner of Breadmarket Street and Market Street on 18 September 1709, the son of the owner of a parchment factory. The Johnsons were prosperous, the house being claimed at the time as the best in Lichfield, though the prosperity was not to last. Samuel reports that as his father's fortunes declined, his eccentricities (always a feature of a somewhat endearing man) increased. When, due to lack of money, the back wall of the parchment factory collapsed, Samuel's father still dutifully locked the front door each night when he left work.

The young Samuel was baptised in St Mary's Church in Market Square, educated at Dame Oliver's School, on the corner of Dam Street and Quonians Lane, a site passed along the Way, and Lichfield Grammar School, before going up to Pembroke College, Oxford, though he left before completing his degree. He began writing while working as usher at Market Bosworth Grammar School and continued after opening his own school at Burntwood. His best-known work, the *Dictionary of the English Language* was published in 1755. After an absence of more than twenty years he visited Lichfield in 1761, and continued to visit the town regularly until his death in 1784. Samuel Johnson is buried in Westminster Abbey. Though his writings would have made Johnson famous in literary circles, James Boswell's record of his wit and insights has elevated him to the position of national treasure. It was Johnson who claimed that marrying a second time was

The spires of Lichfield Cathedral, a local landmark known as 'The Ladies of the Vale', are best viewed across the Minster Pool.

the triumph of hope over experience, that the man who was tired of London was tired of life, and that 'when a man knows he is to be hanged in a fortnight, it concentrates his mind wonderfully'. But a more wayfaring quote is needed for a book such as this. Johnson was not much given to taking exercise, nor to a passionate love of nature. Once he was asked by Boswell if he did not think something was worth seeing (it was the Giant's Causeway, but that is irrelevant to the point Johnson made). 'Worth seeing?' Johnson replied.' Yes, but not worth going to see.' Thus in just a handful of words, the great man identified the difference between those that explore and those who do not.

CANNOCK CHASE

To the north of Meriden there is a subtle change in the landscape, the patches of woodland that were once the Forest of Arden becoming less frequent. By the time the Tame Valley is reached the change is complete, the flat, fertile valley and flooded gravel pits at Kingsbury being a complete contrast to the Arden landscape.

The next change occurs beyond Lichfield, which stands on the western border of the Tame Valley. Here the Way rises on to a plateau of heathland, the remnant of the ancient Cannock Forest.

The Royal Forest of Cannock in which Henry II hunted was a much larger area than the present open land, extending from Tamworth to Wolverhampton, from Walsall to the Trent. As with Arden, Cannock would not have been completely wooded, its stands of oak trees were separated by more open country. In 1290 the hunting rights in the Forest passed, together with the royal estates, to the Bishops of Lichfield. The name changed too, the area becoming the Bishop's Chase, a chase being the medieval term for a hunting area. The fallow and red deer that were the chief quarry of the bishop still roam the Chase, though the reds, the larger animals, are now confined to the southern part of the area. In much more recent times muntjac deer have also colonised the Chase. There are also red squirrels, this being one of the few places in southern England where this delightful animal can still be found. Much of the Chase has been colonised by the reds' American grey cousins, but as much encouragement as possible is being given to the reds in the hope that the remnant population will thrive.

In time the Bishop's Chase of Cannock became Cannock Chase. As at Arden, the sixteenth and seventeenth centuries saw the destruction of the forest: bark was needed to tan the leather of Stafford's shoemakers and then charcoal was needed to fire the Black Country's

Cannock Chase has numerous wildlife habitats, including heath, forest and bog. Small ponds such as this one, are home to rare marshland plants.

furnaces. But unlike that of Arden, the Cannock soil was not fertile, and apart from sheep grazing no farming was carried on after the felling of the oak glades. Today the Chase's heath is covered with bracken and heather, with some patches of grass and wildflowers. There are also crowberries and a hybrid of the crowberry and the bilberry, relatively common (though localized) here, but rare elsewhere, and known as Cannock Chase Berry.

The heath is an acidic, poorly drained land, though much of Cannock Chase is actually quite dry. Where it is wetter, sedges, some rare wetland grasses and bog plants thrive. In 1958, to protect all the heath species, the Chase was designated an Area of Outstanding Natural Beauty (AONB). At around 25 sq miles (65 sq kms) Cannock is Britain's smallest AONB but despite this it includes a large number of Sites of Special Scientific Interest (SSSI) set up to protect the plant and wildlife, among which are some rare birds – including goldcrests, crossbills and hobbies.

Parts of the Chase are now planted with Corsican pine as a commercial crop, the tree having been found to fare better than the native Scots pine in the Chase's poor soil. While opinions will obviously differ, it does seem that the Forestry Commission has trodden a reason-

Cannock Chase has a long military history, but the most poignant memorial is that to the victims of the massacre in Poland's Katyn Forest.

able path between the needs of commerce and those of the natural environment, planting not only the alien pines, but also oak, birch, beech and other native broadleaves.

The history of the Chase is largely that of the hunting forest and its destruction for charcoal, but there are ruins which, though separated by two millenia, are remarkably similar in their use of the landscape. On the Chase's south-eastern corner, where the Way reaches the forest, stands Castle Ring, an Iron Age hill fort commanding the highest point of the Chase (at 801 feet / 244m). About 2,000 years later Cannock Chase saw defences designed to keep people in rather than out when a German prisoner of war camp was constructed during the 1914-18 War. There were also two large British army camps and a hospital, and military training was carried out across the area. Such training, including tank testing, continued until the end of the 1939-45 War. Legacies of the military camps, in addition to the odd ruin, are the Commonwealth and German Military Cemeteries close to the Way at the Chase's western edge. The ominously named Deadman's Walk connected the Commonwealth Cemetery to the 1914-18 hospital on Brindley Heath. Two later memorials have continued the Chase's long association with the military. Close to the Marquis Drive Visitor Centre (itself built on the site of the old RAF Hednesford Camp), and passed along the Way, is a beautiful copse planted by the Burma Star Association as a memorial to local men who died in Burma, while also along the Way – but a little closer to Milford – is the Katyn Memorial raised to the memory of the Polish Officers who were murdered by Stalin's army in Katyn Forest in 1940.

A structure of a much different kind, one which dominates much of the last stages of the Way, is the 285 foot (79m) sculpture-like Post Office Tower at Pye Green.

THE
HEART OF
ENGLAND
WAY

1 BOURTON-ON-THE-WATER TO CHIPPING CAMPDEN

via Lower Slaughter and Longborough 16 miles (25.6 km)

On a warm, sunny weekend day in summer, the centre of Bourton-on-the-Water can be so crowded that the beauty of the place is obscured. Unlike most other Cotswold villages, Bourton plays the tourist game. There is no quiet understatement here, no resigned acceptance of the visitors. Bourton welcomes them all, and puts on a show for each one. But beneath the tourist façade – the Perfumery, the Model Village, the Motor Collection, the Model Railway and much else besides – there is a village of real beauty, its cottages set along the banks of the Windrush, the most 'Cotswold' of all the Cotswold rivers. The river, wide, shallow and duck-paddled, is crossed by little footbridges built, it seems, as much for photographers as for the convenience of villagers.

From the centre of Bourton **1**, go north-westwards along the High Street (in which stands the quaintly named Old New Inn) to reach the church, on the right **2**. The original Norman church, which stood on Saxon foundations, was largely demolished in 1784 and rebuilt with a dome, a unique feature in the Cotswolds. Follow the metalled path to the left of the church, ignoring all turnings, to reach a road.

Turn left to reach a T-junction with the main road. Turn right for about 160 yards, then cross, with care, and go through a gate. Follow the distinct track beyond through several gates to reach a road in Lower Slaughter **3**. Turn left, following the River Eye to a cross roads, with the village church on your right.

The main village of Lower Slaughter lies ahead, a village which has some claim to be the prettiest in the Cotswolds, a claim enhanced by the car-free walk beside the stream, passing delightful stone cottages, that visitors can enjoy. At the end of walk is an old mill, complete with an occasionally moving waterwheel. The mill, now a museum of milling and a crafts showroom, has a brick chimney which, strangely, seems in no way incongruous.

Turn right, passing the church on your right, and, soon, take a short path on the right to a drive. Bear right, passing a lovely house on the left, to reach a path, also on the left. Follow this, initially between walls, to a gate. Now follow the hedge on the right, with the village cricket ground on your left, to a stile/gate and continue beside the hedge to reach a gate in it. Go through and turn left, maintaining

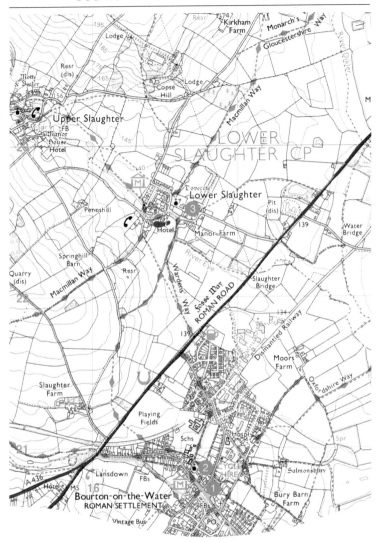

direction, but now with the hedge on your left. In the corner, bear right to reach a squeezer stile on the left. Bear half-left to a gate and then head towards a farm, using the prominent silo as a guide, to reach a gate/squeezer stile. Go half-right, walking about 20 yards from the right-hand field edge to reach a gate in the far hedge. Bear half-right along a tractor track, crossing a stile and continuing to a gate. Now bear slightly right to reach a stile by a stream. The marsh marigolds here are a brilliant splash of colour in spring. Cross a ditch to follow the track to a kissing gate. Ahead, on the hill, is Nether Swell Manor **4**, an imposing building in Cotswold stone.

Turn right over a bridge and follow the track to a gate. Turn left past the houses. The track then bears right to reach a bridge at Hide Mill, but the route goes left through a gate **A** and then through another. Maintain direction, going uphill with a new wooden fence on the right, to reach a barrier and, soon, a gate to a bridleway enclosed by (electric) fences. Follow this to a barrier, and then a gate, on to a track. Follow the track to a road and turn right to a T-junction. Turn right to reach the green at Lower Swell **5**, a village which, along with its 'Upper' neighbour, is named from a shortening of 'Our Lady's Well'.

Bear left, passing the bus shelter to reach a cross roads. Go straight ahead, uphill, then turn right along a track just before 'Church Piece', following it to a stile at its end. Cross and follow the wall on the right to where it turns sharp right. Now bear half-right, downhill, towards the furthest right of the tall trees ahead. Beyond the trees a lake can be glimpsed. Go over a stile and turn left along a drive, passing the lake, followed by houses on the right, and, beyond, a single house on the left. Soon after, go through a kissing gate on the left and head for the power pole to the right of a prominent tree. Bear left along the edge of a cropped area, following an old hedge line of which only some fine oaks now remain. Go downhill to a kissing gate, then along the right-hand edge of a field to another kissing gate. Walk with a fence on the left and a wall on the right, to reach a kissing gate and go around right for 3 yards to reach a squeezer stile on the left.

Cross two paddocks linked by a squeezer stile in a wooden fence to reach two gates on to a road at Upper Swell **6**. Turn left, uphill, ignoring a turning on the left. Now take a turning on the right, going downhill to cross a stream. Follow the road uphill, passing the Donnington Brewery **7** on the left to reach a T-junction.

It was at Donnington village, a short distance to the east, and not on the Way, that Lord Astley surrendered his army in 1646 after the final battle of the first Civil War. Astley is famous for the prayer he composed before the Battle of Edgehill:

Lord I shall be verie busie this day
I may forget Thee, but doe not Thou forget me

Astley had reached Stow on his way to join the king at Oxford. At his surrender Astley was a sorry picture: 'taken captive and wearyed in his fight, and being ancient — for old age's silver haires had quite covered over his head and beard . . . his soldiers brought him a Drum to sit and rest himselfe upon,' Astley told his Parliamentarian captors 'to sit downe and play, for you have done all your worke,' adding, prophetically, 'if you fall not out among yourselves.'

Donnington Brewery grows its own barley and produces beer that, when bottled, requires skilful pouring, as it also contains old-fashioned sediment. The beer can be sampled at many local inns.

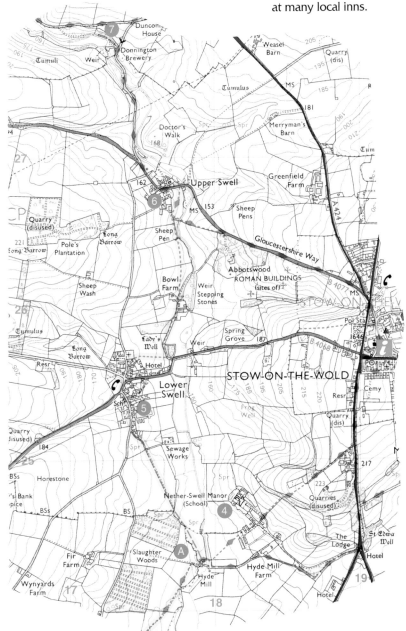

At the T-junction **B** turn right and, soon, go ahead along a lane when the main road bears left. Follow the lane to the main road. Cross, with care, and take the green lane opposite, following it through a fine crop of cow parsley. At its end **C** there are stiles leading left, right and ahead. On my last visit someone had altered the waymarkers in an attempt to confuse the wayfarer. Do not be fooled: go over the stile on the left and follow a faint field path to a stiled bridge. Longborough is now in sight: head towards it, following the edge of a field to a way-marker post. Bear right to follow the hedge on the right, going down-hill through a thicket to reach a bridge and, soon after, a stile. Follow a line of oaks ahead to reach a stile, then the fence on the left to reach another. Continue beside the fence on the left, soon going ahead along a track to reach a gate/stone stile. Follow the track ahead, continuing along a road to reach the sloping green at Longborough **8**.

Bear right below the green, passing a spring plunging from a pipe in a wall, then continue along the street of lovely houses to reach a T-junction. Turn left, passing the village war memorial and a road to the church on the right. The church **9** houses the tomb of Sir Charles Cockerell who built Sezincote, the next objective on the Way. Here, at least, Sir Charles is outdone, the tomb of Sir William Leigh, who died two centuries earlier, being far more elaborate.

About 5 yards beyond the War Memorial, turn right through a gate and follow a path past allotments to a gate. Follow the fence on the right to another gate, then the wall on the right to a hedge gap. Continue past a small conifer plantation, going through a gate, then following the fence/wall on the left. Cross a track to a kissing gate and continue between walls. When the wall on the right turns right **D** go ahead to the first oak and bear half-right, downhill, towards the lake to reach a gate beside a cattle trough. Maintain direction, with Sezincote House **10** uphill to your left, to reach a gate.

Sezincote was remodelled in the early eighteenth century by Sir Charles Cockerell whose wealth derived from his work with the East India Company. He obviously enjoyed the East, and had the house constructed in Mogul (rather than Hindu) Indian style with oriental gardens, though there were concessions to the British climate – in addition to the onion dome there are chimney stacks. The park sur-rounding the house was the work of Humphrey Repton and extends the Indian theme, with cast-iron Brahmin bulls, Hindu goats, and clumps of bamboo. The Prince Regent visited Sezincote in 1807, and it is almost certain that it influenced his plans for the Brighton Pavilion.

Continue for 10 yards to reach another gate, then bear half-right with the fence. Where the fence goes right, maintain direction uphill towards the trees with fence protectors. Follow the waymarkers on the tree stumps, maintaining direction across a drive to the house to reach a kissing gate and, soon after, another. Maintain direction towards the

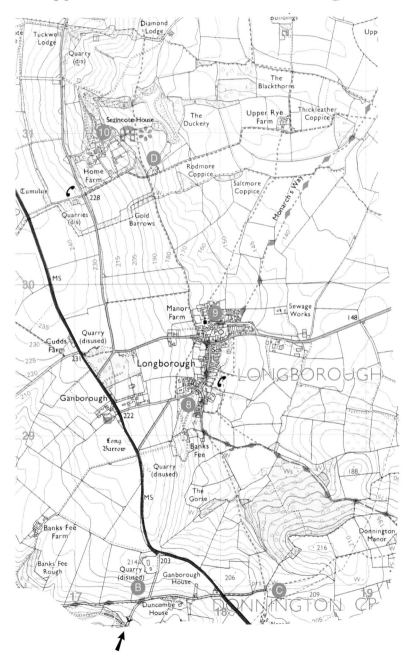

village of Bourton-on-the-Hill, now seen ahead, crossing a stile and going through two gates to reach an enclosed path. Follow this to a road. Turn right, then bear left at the junction, soon passing steps on the left that lead up to the church **11**, in which there is a rare survival – a Winchester bushel and peck. Before 1587 the system of weights and measures in Britain was haphazard, but in that year Elizabeth I granted a charter to Winchester making the city's official weights and measures Britain's standard. Magistrates' clerks throughout the country had to obtain standard weights and measures. The Bourton set are dated 1816, making them very rare: in 1826 Imperial standards replaced Winchester standards and the two pieces became obsolete.

Continue along the lane to its T-junction with the main road. Turn right for about 700 yards (650m), passing, on the right, a superb tithe barn, one of the biggest in the area. Now cross the road, with care, and turn left along the entrance drive to the Batsford Estate **12** where there is an aboretum and falconry centre. The arboretum – considered the finest private collection of rare trees and shrubs in Britain – was the creation of Lord Redesdale, the British Ambassador to Japan in the mid-nineteenth century. The falconry centre has flying demonstrations by eagles, owls, hawks and falcons.

Curiously, the right of way is not continuous along the drive, though since the drive is the entrance to the visitor sites it is difficult to see anyone objecting to its use. Strictly though, the Way follows the drive for about 450 yards (400m), then goes right over a stile **E**, bears half-left to the field corner, then turns sharp left along the field edge to return to the drive. Go through the gate opposite and uphill along a faint path to reach a stile. Cross and walk ahead for 10 yards to join a track. Bear left, uphill, for about 450 yards (400m), then take the track **F** (the first reached) on the right following it to a gate. Do not go through: instead, turn left to walk beside a wall on your right, following it past a gate on the right and a jump for cross-country events to reach a gate to a road. Bear right across the road and go along a track, soon reaching two gates. Take the right-hand gate and follow the left edge of the fields beyond, going through another gate and passing excellent horse chestnut, ash, sycamore and beech trees, then going through a gate to reach a wonderful view of Blockley nestling in the valley below.

Turn left through a gate and continue for about 100 yards to reach a stile on the right **G**. Cross and follow the right-hand field edge downhill until a farm comes into view, then bear slightly left to reach a stile in the extreme bottom corner. Bear half-right to a track and maintain direction across it, heading towards a power pole with a huge footpath sign and continuing to a gate/stile. Follow the hedge on the right to a stile, and the track beyond to a road. Turn left, uphill, then first right, descending and bearing left. At the bottom of the hill, turn first right (up a 'No Through Road'), going steeply up to a T-junction. Turn right through an exquisite part of Blockley **13** to reach a cross roads with the church ahead.

Blockley is, arguably, the most unspoilt of the larger Cotswold villages. It, too, suffered from the decline of the woollen industry, but its folk benefited from Knee Brook, the fast flowing stream in its secluded valley which powered silk mills producing raw ribbon for the Coventry ribbon factories.

One of the most unspoilt of Cotswold villages is Blockley, seen to perfection from th

ay as it descends in to the valley of the Knee Brook.

The Way passes through the pretty hamlet of Broad Campden, passing cottages of warm stone, their small front gardens coloured with summer flowers.

Turn sharp left, away from the church. This narrow steep road is Bell Bank, but the nameplate is at the top end. Follow the road to a T-junction (and nameplate) and turn right to reach another T-junction. Cross straight over and follow a path beside a fence (of the doctors' surgery, to the left) to a stile. Maintain direction to a hedge gap and cross a track to a stile. Now head for the delightful barn on the hillside on the far side of the valley below, descending steeply to reach a gate/stile by a stream **H**. Maintain direction to the hedge ahead and walk with it on your right, climbing to the field corner. (Do not go through the gate on the right.) Go through a gate, a sheep-shearing pen and another gate, then through a hedge gap. Soon, turn left through a gate and follow a path through a glorious patch of rosebay willowherb (grossly underrated in Britain, even to the extent of being called a weed, but the National Flower of Greenland) to reach a field. Follow the hedge on the left to reach a surfaced track (from Hangman's Hall Farm, off to the right) and maintain direction along it for about 650 yards (600m) to reach a track junction at the Five Mile Drive **I**.

Turn right, taking the second track on the right. It is signed 'Beware – Two-Way Traffic' and is heading north-west. The track is flat at first, then goes downhill and curves left to reach Campden Hill Farm. Just before the farm **J** turn right through a gate and go uphill (with a barn to the left and a pond to the right) to reach a gate. Do not go through: instead, bear right, with a wall on your left, and follow an undulating path over stiles to reach some railings. Go between the railings, to your right, and the wall to where the railings go sharp right **K**. Here, bear half-right, downhill to an intermittent hedge. Go through this and bear left to reach a stile. Cross a short section of fenced grass and bear right towards the houses (of Broad Campden) to reach a fence corner. Continue with the fence on your right to the field corner, turning left there to reach a gate leading on to the road at Broad Campden **14**.

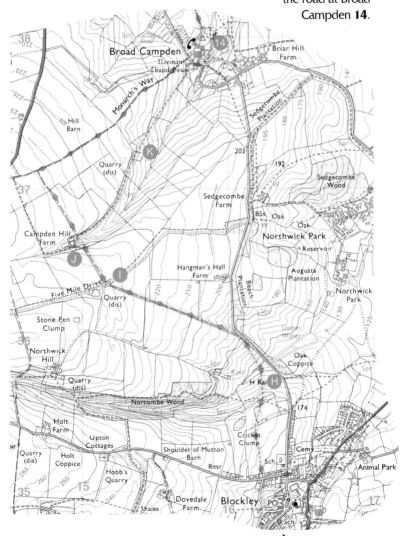

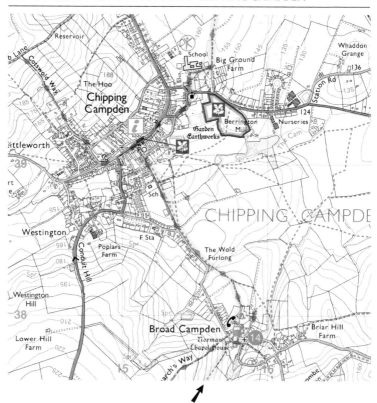

Turn right, passing the Baker's Arms to reach a road junction by the church. Turn sharp left along the 'No Through Road' (not along the lane beside the church) passing some very pretty cottages. At the end of the lane, take the narrow path on the left, between walls, to a kissing gate. Continue to reach a drive between staddle stones. The stones were originally used as the damp- and rodent-proof foundations for barns, but are now more often seen as decoration. Cross the drive and go between two more staddle stones, following the fence on the left to a kissing gate. You are crossing the garden of the house to the right: please be considerate. Maintain direction across the field beyond, walking with a low wall on your right. When the wall ends, bear left, downhill, to reach a fence beside a road. Bear right and follow the fence on your left, then take two steps left to reach the road. Turn right along George Lane, passing tennis courts to the left. When you reach a road, continue ahead, gently downhill, and, at the bottom bear left through the car park and archway of the Noel Arms Hotel to reach High Street, Chipping Campden.

Chipping Campden's High Street, one of the best in the Cotswolds, framed by the arcades of the Market Hall.

CIRCULAR WALK FROM LOWER SLAUGHTER

2½ miles (4km)

From the church at Lower Slaughter, walk westwards, with the River Eye on your left and an array of lovely houses on your right. Ignore the little footbridges over the river, following the narrowing path around a corner to reach the Old Mill with its brick chimney stack and waterwheel. Turn left beyond the shop, going through two kissing gates (signed for the Wardens' Way) and walking with the river on your left. Go through a kissing gate, and bear half-right to another. Cross the field beyond to yet another kissing gate, then bear half-right along a faint path to reach a gate on to a road **A**. Turn left, but before the road crosses a bridge turn right over a stile and follow a path across marshland to reach a stile. Cross it to reach the wonderfully picturesque ford at Upper Slaughter **15**. There is a fine dovecote up-river, but the walk turns left over the bridge beside the ford: walk up

Upper Slaughter's most picturesque feature is the ford of the Slaughterbrook.

the hill into the centre of the village, with the church on the right. The church has been 'modernised' several times, not always successfully, but is still worth visiting. One rector was the Reverend F.E. Witts who wrote *The Diary of a Cotswold Parson*. At the T-junction, where the grassed section is little more than a small reminder of a village green, the Lords of the Manor Hotel is ahead. Upper Slaughter has two manor houses. The original one is a largely Elizabethan house built on earlier foundations; with its row of dormer windows and Jacobean doorway, it has been described as the most beautiful domestic house in the Cotswolds, but sadly, the manor is not, at present, open to the public. The other manor was the old parsonage, but took a new name in the nineteenth century when the rector became Lord of the Manor. It is now the hotel. Turn left and go around a left-hand bend **B** to reach a footpath on the right, signed for the Wardens' Way. Follow this to a clapper bridge over the River Eye and bear right to reach a kissing gate passed on the outward route. Retrace the outward route to the next kissing gate, then bear half-left to reach a gate into a spinney. Go through the spinney and a kissing gate to reach an enclosed path and follow it through kissing gates to reach a lane. Go ahead, following the lane back to the church in Lower Slaughter.

2 CHIPPING CAMPDEN TO BIDFORD-ON-AVON

via Upper Quinton and Long Marston   *14 miles (22.4 km)*

Chipping Campden **16** is the perfect Cotswold town, its warm-stoned buildings being both the finest example of their kind and a mirror of the history of the area. To the left at the point where the Way enters the town is Sheep Street, where the Old Silk Mill houses the town's famous Guild of Handicrafts, founded by C.R. Ashbee 1902.

Turn right along Chipping Campden High Street, soon passing the Town Hall and Market Hall on the left. Legend has it that the Town Hall incorporates the remains of a chapel built by Hugh de Gondeville, a local man who led the gang which murdered Thomas à Becket, in an attempt to expunge his guilt. The Market Hall was given to the town by Sir Baptist Hicks 'for the sale of butter, cheese and poultry'. Continue along the High Street, passing Woolstapler's Hall to the right. The Hall is fourteenth century and was the meeting place of the staple (i.e. sheep fleece) merchants. Almost opposite is Grevel's House, built in the late fourteenth-century for William Grevel, one of the richest merchants of the time. A memorial brass to Grevel and his wife can be seen in the town church. Though he was a Cotswold man, Grevel is thought to have been the model for Chaucer's merchant in *The Canterbury Tales*.

Beyond Grevel's House is the old water pump. Ahead from here, just a short distance, is the Ernest Wilson Memorial Garden, planted in memory of a Campden-born man responsible for the introduction of thousands of oriental shrubs and trees to the west. 'Chinese' Wilson, as he was known, became director of the famous Arnold Arboretum at Harvard University in the late 1920s.

Just before the water pump, turn right along Church Street, passing the fourteenth-century Eight Bells Inn to reach the town's Almshouses which stand on a raised pavement to the left. The houses were another benefaction of Sir Baptist Hicks who had them built in 1612, at a cost of £1,000, to house six poor men and six poor women. To the right as you continue up Church Street is a reminder of old country ways. The curious trench is a walled dip. Once water-filled, the dip would have been used to clean the wheels of carts arriving at Campden's market, and also to expand the wooden wheels during dry weather so that spokes would not rattle and come loose, or the wooden rim shrink and shed its iron hoop.

Among the many bequests Sir Baptist Hicks made to Chipping Campden was the Market Hall, erected in the early sixteenth century.

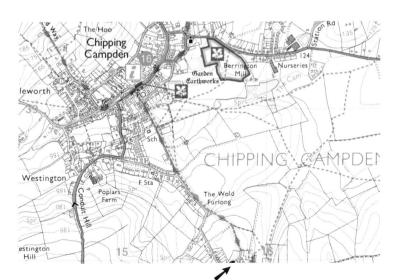

Alabaster effigies of the wool merchant Sir Baptist Hicks and his wife Elizabeth lie on their tomb in St James' Church, Chipping Campden.

Ahead now is the elaborate gateway of Campden House. This, too, was built by Sir Baptist Hicks. Hicks was a London wool merchant who moved to the Cotswolds and became fabulously rich, endowing the church, the Market Place and Almshouses; he also built houses in London on what is now Campden Hill Square in Kensington. Campden House was of such ostentatious splendour that the locals took exception to it, despite being used to occasional shows of wealth by rich merchants. In comparison to the Market Hall which cost Hicks £90, he spent £29,000 on his house and a further £15,000 on furnishings. When the House was garrisoned by Royalist forces in 1645 (about 30 years after its completion), there was a mysterious fire and it was completely destroyed.

Beyond the gateway is St James's Church, one of the finest 'wool' churches in the Cotswolds, the churches being so-called because they were endowed by the rich wool merchants of the day. The church has a 120 foot (36m) tower topped by twelve pinnacles representing the twelve Apostles. Inside are the Grevel brass and the huge, ostentatious tombs of the Hicks' family, which virtually fill the south chapel. There are life-size alabaster effigies of Sir Baptist and Lady Elizabeth Hicks lying in coronation robes, the pair overlooked by the figures of their eldest daughter (Juliana) and her husband (Sir Edward Noel) in funeral shrouds, hand-in-hand, arising from their tomb on judgment day. Much more delicate is the memorial to Penelope Hicks, a daughter of Sir Edward and Juliana, who died of blood poisoning when just 22 years old after pricking her finger on an embroidery needle.

Follow the road past the church to reach an angled T-junction. Turn right for a few yards, then go left along a drive. After about 50 yards go through an undistinguished iron gate on the right **A** and follow a narrow, overgrown path, overshadowed by trees, past gardens on the right, and (after a sharp right-hand bend) a school on the left. The path ends at a field: go left along its edge and keep ahead, with a hedge on your left, to reach a corner. Go right for a few yards, then left over a stile and bear right along a narrow path (with a hedge on your right). The field is a touring caravan site in summer, so you may have some company.

As you approach Mickleton Hills Farm you are walking above the Worcester to Oxford railway line **17** which enters the Campden Tunnel in the aptly-named Tunnel Plantation, about half a mile (800m) to the north, and emerges just a few yards to your right. Bear left to pass the farm on your right and go through a gate, heading almost due north along an avenue of fine horse chestnuts and the occasional oak.

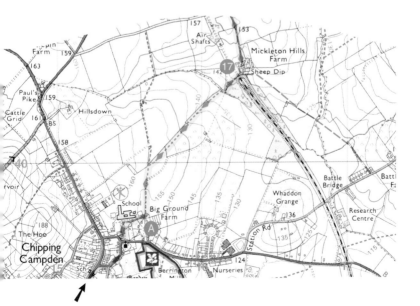

As walkers leave the churchyard in Mickleton they will be surprised by this magnificent view of a typical Cotswold manor house.

The lane ends at a road: turn right for about 400 yards, then go first left (signed as a footpath for Mickleton) along a lane. Follow the lane for about 990 yards (900m) to reach a prominent black Dutch barn on the left **B**. Go left here, then immediately right along a signed path for Mickleton, walking with a hedge on your right. Follow the path into a delightful piece of mixed woodland, its marvellous big beeches scrawled with graffiti. There are bluebells here in spring and other wild-flowers later. When the path reaches a field, follow the left-hand edge to a gate and stile. Beyond, the path descends steeply to a lane (Baker's Hill). Cross to a gate and follow the right-hand edge of the field beyond (with woodland on your right). When the wood ends **C** maintain direction towards the bottom right-hand corner where a stile is tucked away on the right. Cross it and turn left, with a hedge on your left and Mickleton Church soon appearing ahead. Go through a gate and head for the superb oak tree, maintaining direction to reach a track between stone walls that emerges beside the church **18**.

Turn right up the ramp towards the church, passing it on your right to follow a faint path across the churchyard to a stile. Cross it and follow the walled ditch on the left. Beyond the ditch there is a magnificent building set behind a manicured lawn. Go through a gate and follow a track to a road. Turn left for a few yards, then cross to the butchers' shop **D**. Facing the shop, take the narrow (and unlikely) alley to its right to reach a playing field. At this point do not cross to the obvious stile ahead, but follow the right-hand edge of the playing field to reach an (as yet unseen) stile on the right. Cross this and the field beyond to reach a stile on to a main road. Cross and follow
the rough track beyond

B4632 Weston-sub-Edge
3 km or 2 miles

towards Meon Hill **19**. The hill is the last outlier of the Cotswolds, its existence due to differential erosion which has separated it from the main Cotswold mass to the south. Not surprisingly, in view of its commanding position, the hill was the site of an Iron Age fort covering 24 acres from which a hoard of iron currency bars was excavated in the nineteenth century. On St Valentine's Day 1945 it was the scene of a horrific murder, a local farm labourer being found pinned to the flank of the hill with his own pitchfork, through his throat. Despite long investigations, the murder remains unsolved amid local gossip about witchcraft and Satanic rites.

When the track bears left, continue ahead to pass to the right of two sheds. Cross a short bridge and stile and walk across a field to a gate. Cross another arable field to reach a gate and stile. Follow a delightful short hawthorn hedge, on your right to reach a stile on the right. Cross it and go uphill, soon reaching a stile on the left leading into a pleasant section of woodland. Cross a stile and a field, passing two magnificent oaks, then cross two stiles in quick succession (with the fine farm at Lower Clopton down to your left). Now follow the hawthorn hedge, with occasional oaks, on the left to reach a stile, on the left. Cross and turn right beside the hedge. After about 150 yards

The Way goes around the eastern flank of Meon Hill, the last Cotswold outlier.

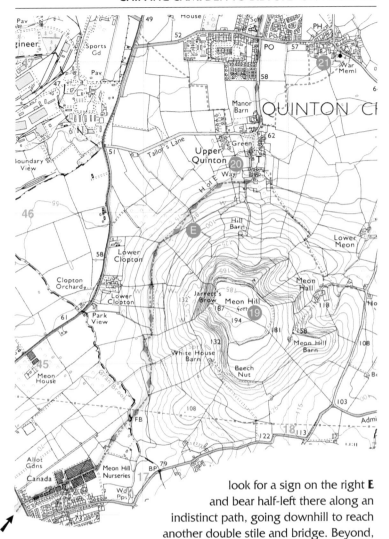

look for a sign on the right **E** and bear half-left there along an indistinct path, going downhill to reach another double stile and bridge. Beyond, follow the hedge on the left across a hummocky field, but where the hedge turns left, go half-right to reach a stile and sign telling you that you should have stayed on the (not obvious) path as the field is not dedicated to walkers. Cross the stile and a rough field to reach a lane. Go ahead, bearing left with the lane to reach the green at Upper Quinton **20** passing the Centenary Way on the right.

Follow the lane across the green to a T-junction and turn right to reach a T-junction at Lower Quinton. The village church, St Swithun's, an ominous dedication if it is raining on your walk, lies to the right **21**.

Although usually following field paths, the Way across the edge of the Vale of Evesham occasionally uses broader paths, as here near Long Marston.

Cross the road and bear left for a few metres **F**. Do not take the lane here: instead, go through the gate into the Primary School grounds. The right of way now follows the right edge of the grounds, with classrooms full of children to your left. Leap past the long-jump pit and race along the marked sprint lanes to reach a stile and bridge into a field. Cross to a well-hidden plank bridge (beware: the field edge is overgrown and it is easy to miss the bridge. The ditch it crosses will then not be missed). Cross a stile and another field to an odd, galvanised bridge and stile. Turn left, walking with a hedge, and then a ditch, on your left, and crossing two stiles to reach a gate on to the B4632.

Cross to the stile opposite. Bear slightly left to reach a fence and bear right to walk with it on your left until you reach a gate on the left. Go through and, soon, turn right over a low stile. Turn left to another stile and then go right, with a hedge on your right, to the corner. Turn left, still with the hedge on your right. Beyond the hedge is a disused airfield, part of which has been taken over by the Avon Park Raceway. Continue with the hedge on your right, crossing a bridge and stile and going through a gate. Now maintain direction (with a truly unmistakable sewage farm to the right) to reach a gate on to a track. There are some very fine willows on the right here and, usually, a flock of sheep who grudgingly yield the track as you follow it to a gate and an old railway. Continue along the track and, where a road joins from the right, walk ahead to reach a T-junction in Long Marston **22**.

In Shakepeare's famous drinking poem (which will be mentioned again as several other villages noted in it are passed before Bidford, the scene of the action behind the poem, is reached) the village is 'Dancing Marston', though why this should be is not certain. About a century ago the village had a famous team of Morris Men, described as being 'fantastically decked with ribbons ... bells attached to their legs ... (and) ... accompanied by a tabor and piper ... and a Motley fool.' It is usually assumed that the team were an ancient one, and were the origin of Shakepeare's adjective. Long Marston has a strange royal connection, King Charles II spent a night here, at the home of the Tomes family, in 1651. Charles (king in name only at the time) was making his escape to France and nine years of exile after the battle of Worcester. Travelling as the manservant of Jane Lane, the king was sent to help in the kitchen where the cook, a formidable lady who was unaware of his true identity (which had been revealed to no one), boxed his ears when he proved to be incompetent at managing the roasting spit. One version of the story has it that the incident occurred in front of a squad of Parliamentarian soldiers who were searching the house as the Tomes family were known to be royalist sympathisers.

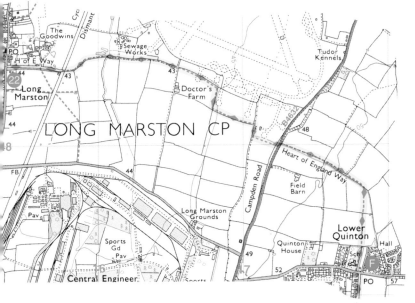

At the T-junction, turn right for about 60 yards to reach a Methodist Chapel on the left. Facing the chapel **G** go along the path/drive to its right, turning right to go between splendid black and white cottages to reach a short section of path overgrown with nettles passing a house on the left. Most walkers reach the field beyond the house by way of the inn car park (further along the road past the chapel), but the right of way is through the nettles. Cross the stile into the field, turn left and follow

Waymarking on the route, with the distinctive green and white sign, is usually excellent, as here on a stiled bridge near Dorsington.

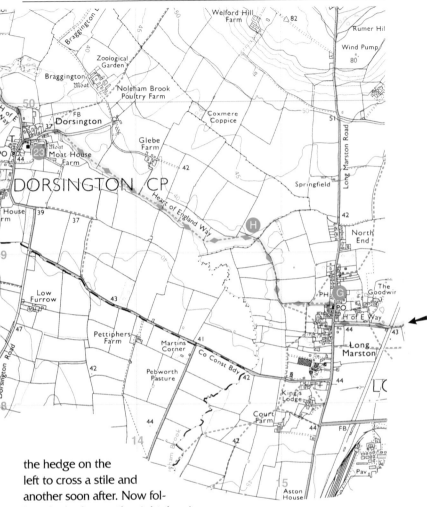

the hedge on the
left to cross a stile and
another soon after. Now follow the hedge on the right, bearing
right in the corner to reach a stile. From here follow the hedge on the
right through several fields to reach a bridge and squeezer stile **H**. From
this point head for the power line pole (signed with a yellow arrow) and
maintain direction to the far hedge. Turn right, with the hedge on your
left, to reach a stile and bridge. Follow the hedge/stream on the left
through a gate and over two stiles to a road.

Turn left to reach Dorsington **23** passing a beautiful thatched, half-
timbered cottage on the right. At the T-junction, with the simple village
church (built in red and yellow brick in 1758) to the left and a splendid
house ahead, turn right along the road towards Bidford-on-Avon.

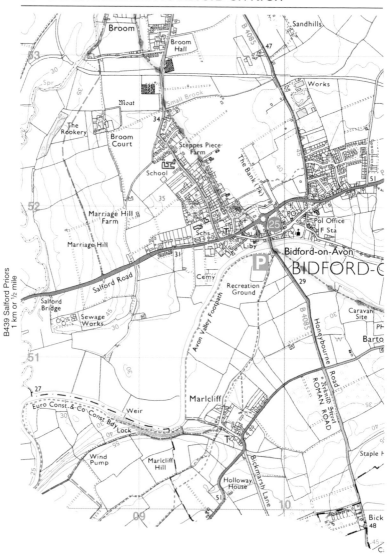

Follow the road around left, right and left bends, then, at the next right-hand bend, go ahead through a gate and along a track. After 275 yards (250m), where the track turns left by three gates (one to the left and two to the right), go through the first right-hand gate and follow the hedge on the left to reach a stile on the left. Cross, bear right over a bridge and walk with the hedge on your left to reach the top of the field. Turn left and follow the hedge on the right. Pass a wide track leading off to the right, then turn right (still with a hedge on your right)

and head uphill to the now-visible Barton Farm **I**. Bear left at the farm with the buildings on your right, to reach the farm drive. Turn left and follow the drive to the road in Barton **24**. Bear right along the road to where it turns sharp right. Here take the track ahead, between the Cottage of Content Inn on the left and a small shop on the right. Go over a stile and go up a short slope to reach the Avon. The river here, with its weir and lock, is very beautiful. Go left to walk between a caravan site on the left and a fence bordering the river on the right. Cross a stile and follow the hedge on the right. When it ends, maintain direction, crossing stiles to reach the B4085. As you approach the road the view of Bidford-on-Avon **25** is magnificent: the precise lines of the squat church of St Lawrence, the array of delightful houses beside the river, and the ancient bridge. Turn right to cross the bridge, using the passing places on top of its upstream buttresses to avoid the traffic.

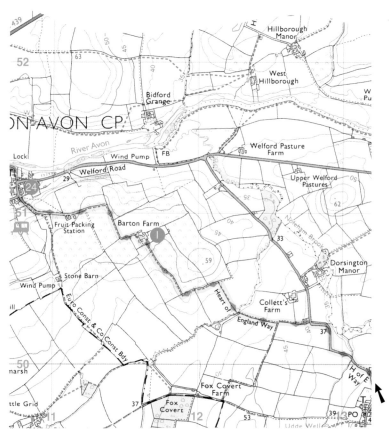

To reach Bidford-on-Avon the Way crosses the fifteenth-century Avon bridge, restore

...er damage by Royalist soldiers and, much later, a combine harvester.

3 BIDFORD-ON-AVON TO HENLEY-IN-ARDEN

via Alcester   *13 miles (20.8 km)*

The Roman Ryknild Street crossed the Avon at Bidford **25**. There may even have been a bridge, though the present bridge with its fine collection of irregular arches was built in the early fifteenth century. It has required repair several times, most particularly after partial destruction by the Royalist army in 1644 seeking to slow the pursuing Roundheads, and again in 1994 when a crossing combine harvester became firmly stuck. From the river the view of the town is as delightful as that from the water meadow approach, the eye being drawn along the line of fine buildings beside the river to the church of St Lawrence, built in 1835 despite its medieval look. The Way turns left after crossing the bridge, but a right turn is worthwhile to see some of the village's really lovely old houses, the church and, best of all, the mullioned and transomed Old Falcon Inn on the corner of High Street and Church Street.

One Whit Monday William Shakespeare and some of his friends went to Bidford to take on the local drinking team, known as the Bidford Topers, in a drinking contest. There appears to have been a mix-up as the Topers had gone to Evesham to compete in a more significant event, leaving the Stratford team to compete against the Bidford 'B' team, known as the Sippers. The Sippers were good enough, though, to drink the Stratford lads under the table, the end of an evening which saw Shakespeare's men making their somewhat unsteady way home. They made it as far as a crab-apple tree under which they collapsed. The next morning Shakespeare, suffering from a hangover, is said to have penned the famous lines which declared that never again would he drink with the men of

Piping Pebworth, Dancing Marston,
Haunted Hillborough, Hungry Grafton,
Dodging Exhall, Papist Wixford,
Beggarly Broom and Drunken Bidford.

In 1824 the crab-apple tree, by then a place of pilgrimage, was still alive (Could it possibly have been the same tree ? and if so had it been kept alive by the vast quantity of alcoholic vapour it had absorbed ?) On 4 December it was transplanted to Bidford Grange, where it promptly died.

From the town end of the bridge, turn left along the High Street to reach the Frog and Bullrush Inn. Here turn right, beside the lovely half-timbered house of 'Independent Financial Advisers', heading towards the Methodist Chapel. Bear right, following the lane past excellent dog roses on the left, to reach the B439. Cross and follow the tarmac path opposite. Bear left along a lane, following it around a right-hand bend and through the houses. Continue along the track ahead to reach a road opposite the Broom Court Farm **26**: the Court has a fine Jacobean portal.

Turn right and follow the road to the humped bridge over a disused railway **27**. The railway was the Redditch and Evesham, which joined the Stratford and Midland Junction Railway, known by its initials of SMJ which, locals maintained, actually stood for Slow Mournful Journey. Interestingly, despite the nickname (and another which claimed the railway was the Slow Man's Joy) the owners were quite innovative. In 1911 they introduced 'Railophone' which allowed the driver and passengers to telephone to a fixed point and in 1932 they created the 'Rorailer', a bus with steel-flanged, rubber-tyred wheels which could travel on both the railway lines and the road. Neither invention came to anything, though the second does seem to have had some definite merits.

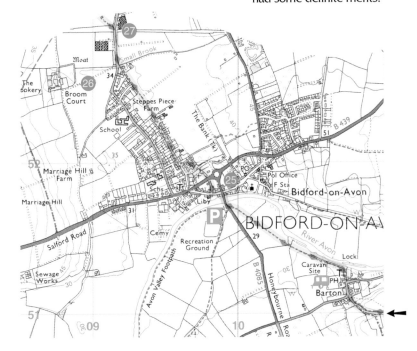

Just over the crown of the bridge **A** go left, downhill through a thicket to reach a field. Follow the fence on the right to a crossing track. Take the track ahead, to the right of the hedge, following it to a road in Broom. Take the road ahead, alongside the Broom Tavern, to reach a T-junction. Go diagonally right along the drive of a beautiful half-timbered house – no part of today's village warrants Shakespeare's description of 'Beggarly Broom' – then follow the narrow path between a hedge on the left, and a wooden fence on the right, to reach a stile. Maintain direction, soon with a hedge on your right, through gates to reach a track. Cross and maintain direction, now with a hedge on your left, to reach a stile on the left. Cross this to reach a raised bank and follow it to a stile and bridge over an inflow stream to the River Arrow, now close by on your left. Follow the wide track ahead to reach a road opposite the Fish Inn **28**. Along this section the Arrow on the walk is very pretty, delightfully shaded and with a view of a weir through the arch of the road bridge.

Cross the road and walk through the inn car park to the caravan site, passing the caravans on your left to reach a stile. Maintain direction to another stile and cross on to an overgrown path. Soon, bear right with the path (do not go ahead into the field) walking with a fence on the right, beyond which is a bottled gas depot. Pass a gate, then ignore a stile on the right. Now pass a house on the left and maintain direction along a track to a T-junction with a lane. To the left is Wixford Church **29,** with one of the largest and finest memorial brasses in Warwickshire, to Thomas de Cruwe, who died in 1411, and his wife. The detail of the wife's dress is superb. Wixford is 'Papist Wixford' in Shakespeare's verse, probably because the local manorial family were the Catholic Throckmortons. The yew in the churchyard is several hundred years old: in 1669 the villagers successfully asked the bishop to put a stop to the vicar's plans to cut down the tree.

Cross the road **B** and go through the gates: the 'Private Drive' sign applies only to vehicles. Follow the drive around a sharp left-hand bend, with Oversley Castle **30** appearing ahead. The site is named for a twelfth-century castle erected by Ralph le Boteler, but the present building is early nineteenth-century, despite the embattled tower. Go around a right-hand bend and follow the drive to reach a track on the left, just before some stout wooden gates. Take the track, following it to the right and then downhill to where another track joins from the left. Bear right, soon passing some lovely ash trees on the right. Pass a house and two barns on the left and a track on the right, then bear left with the track (as another joins from the right) heading towards the two tall silos ahead. Away to your right here is Oversley Wood **31** a remnant of the old Forest of Arden, with mixed deciduous trees and some Corsican pine.

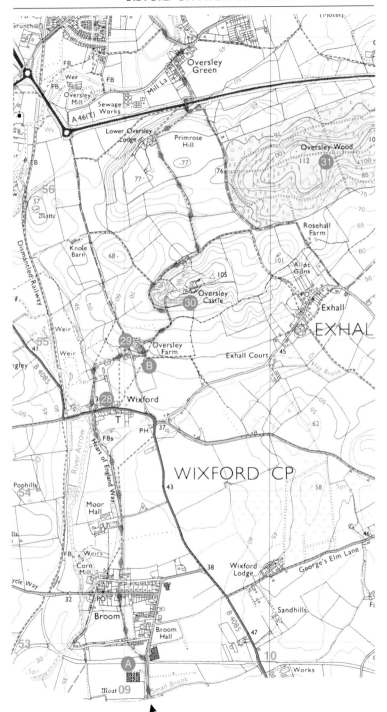

A weir on the River Arrow glimpsed beneath the bridge near the Fish Inn.

The two tall silos are at Lower Oversley Lodge Farm. There are also four squat silos and a variety of barns: clearly some serious farming takes place here. As you pass the farm on your left, the track becomes concrete: bear right with it (away from the farm) walking parallel to the main road below and to the left, with Alcester beyond. Go downhill to reach a stile on the left. Cross to a footbridge over the main road and continue to reach Primrose Lane near a glorious thatched house. Even the garage is thatched!

Follow the lane to a T-junction and turn right on Mill Lane. When Mill Lane reaches a road, turn left and follow the road over a 'weak' bridge to reach a T-junction on the outskirts of Alcester **32**.

Alcester was the Roman *Alauna* built beside the Ryknild Street and defended with a ditch and rampart. The town was also close to a salt way, salt being an important commodity for preserving meat before refrigeration. Later the town was a prosperous market and also a coach stop, being situated at just the right distance from Birmingham for overnight inns to flourish. It was also a centre for malting, leatherwork and for the making of needles. Alcester is a delightful place and one worthy of exploration, though the Way does actually pass most of the more interesting buildings in town. Malt Mill Lane is the most picturesque street in town. The array of timber-framed houses has been carefully restored and is now sheltered housing for senior citizens. The name derives from a malting kiln discovered behind the houses on the eastern side of the lane. Old Mill House, the marvellous building at the town end of the lane, dates from the early fifteenth-century. Close to the town end of the lane is St Nicholas' Church, an early eighteenth-century church erected on the site of a fourteenth-century building, of which the tower is the only survival. The church's most interesting features lie inside: look for the fine Victorian pulpit with its carved panels of the Evangelists; the tomb of the Marquess of Hertford, who appears in effigy, curiously lounging on a couch; the tapestries on the south wall which were made by the townsfolk in the 1980s and illustrate life in Alcester; and, best of all, the tomb of Sir Fulke Greville and his wife Elizabeth. Sir Fulke, who died in 1559, was Lord of the Manor. The effigies are very detailed: Sir Fulke is shown with a sharp beard, while his wife's dress is depicted so well it even allows a peep up her skirts. The mourners (known as 'weepers') around the tomb are the couple's fifteen children. A short distance from the church is the town hall, a sturdy building whose lower storey was built by Sir Fulke Greville in 1618. The lower storey originally had open arcades and served as a market. The hall itself is on the upper storey and was added twenty years later. Behind the hall is Butter Street with some really lovely houses. There are other fine buildings in the High Street, which continues from Butter Street, and in Henley Street, which is the route taken by the Way.

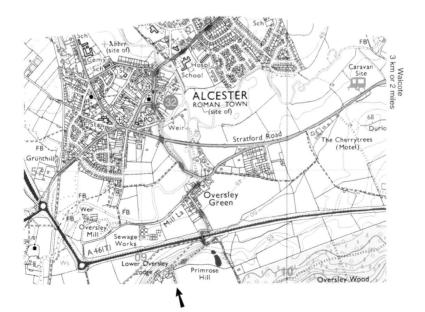

Alcester also has an unlikely place in the history of Arctic exploration. Frederick Jackson, a local man, applied for permission to accompany Nansen on his *Fram* expedition, perhaps the most audacious trip of all time. Nansen planned to freeze the ship in the Arctic pack ice and allow the natural drift of the ice to tow him across the North Pole. Nansen refused Jackson's request. After months trapped in the pack, the Norwegian realised the ship would miss the Pole and set out with another man on skis to reach it. They failed, but missed *Fram* on their journey south, eventually reaching, after an epic journey, the island of Franz Josef. There the two men overwintered. When spring came they despaired of ever being rescued, when Frederick Jackson suddenly appeared in his own ship, *Windward*. The Alcester man had not been searching for Nansen, but took him on board and ferried him safely back to Norway.

Cross the road **C** follow the path through the small park and turn right to reach Malt Mill Lane. Follow the lane to a road and bear right, passing the church, with Butter Street and the town hall on your left. Follow the road (the B4089) out of the town. Where the B4089 goes left to Birmingham and Redditch, continue on for about 90 yards, then go left along a path through woodland. Cross a stile and head uphill to pass a forlorn trig point. Continue slightly downhill to a stile. Bear left, soon reaching another stile on to an overgrown path across a disused railway. Cross a stile and follow the left field edge for about 100 yards to reach a stile on the left. Cross and turn right, with the hedge now on your right, crossing a stile to reach a gate to a lane. Turn left, but soon go right over a stile and head uphill towards woodland. Cross a stile into the wood (near a pond on the right), then cross a rutted track to reach a field. Follow the hedge on the right to reach a gap in it. Go through, turn left and continue with the hedge now on your left, following a narrow path, to reach a bridge/stile on the left. Cross and turn right then, soon, right again over a bridge to reach a stile on to a lane.

Take the track for Dinglewell Farm almost opposite (a little to the left). About 60 yards after the second house on the right **D** go left over a stile and follow a tractor track uphill to a gate/stile. From here follow the hedge on the right to reach a stile on to a road. Turn left, passing a house on the left to reach a sharp, uphill left-hand bend. Here, go right along a track. The wildlife on the next section of the Way is very good. Walkers, particularly early morning walkers in the summer, will see rabbits and pheasants, hear the rippling call of curlews and smell the pungent scent of foxes. Follow the track past two barns, on the left, and then bear left along a green track with a

Modern agriculture is changing not only the look but also the colour of the countryside

Here, near Great Alne, a field of linseed adds a blanket of blue.

The country to the north of Alcester emerges from an early morning mist.

field on the left, and a hedge on the right, to reach woodland. On exiting the trees, follow the woodland edge on your left until it bears away, then maintain direction to reach a stile on the left **E**. Ignore the yellow arrow, following the white arrow/green disc across the long field beyond the stile, heading towards the distant houses to reach a gate on to a lane at Burford Lane Farm **33**.

Turn right to reach a lane on the right. There, turn left along a dreadfully overgrown path – thankfully only 6 yards long – to reach two stiles only a yard apart. Cross these and turn right, with a hedge on your right, crossing a stile and continuing to another. About a yard further on, go through a gate and follow the low hawthorn hedge on the right to reach a gate on the right **F**. There was no defined path across the arable field beyond the gate on my last visit. If that is still the case, aim just to the right of the mid-point of two distant pylons, then for a fence corner when it becomes visible. Follow the fence, keeping it on your right, to reach a stile. Continue with a hedge on the right to a stile into a very good, but very difficult, blackthorn thicket. Go steeply downhill through the thicket to reach a bridge/stile, then uphill towards some fenced nettles (!). Bear half-right at this curious enclosure to reach a gate on to a road.

Turn right, passing the entrance to Greenhill Farm **34**. The 'official' route now follows the road before taking a footpath through Bannam's Wood; but for conservation reasons there is currently a temporary diversion which takes a ladder stile beside a gate on the right. Cross the stile (in summer its intertwining cotoneaster will attract swarms of bees to keep you company) and follow a track to a gate, with a new farmhouse across the field beyond. Go through the gate and turn right, keeping the hedge on your right and passing a curious dried-up pond with seats on the left, and continuing through a gate/stile to reach a gate **G**. Ahead are a series of white marker posts, but the route turns left past a notice stating the position on the permissive path which takes the Way through Bannam's Wood **35**. Please read this carefully.

Despite the notice's suggestion that the path is 'hard by' the edge of the wood, go into the wood with the fence on your left, climbing through it to reach open grass. Now you continue with the wood, to your left. Bannam's is wonderful, a mixed deciduous wood, with ash, hazel, fully matured hawthorn trees, maple and sweet chestnut dominating, but other species too. And if all this was not idyllic enough, the view to the right across Shakespeare's Warwickshire is magnificent.

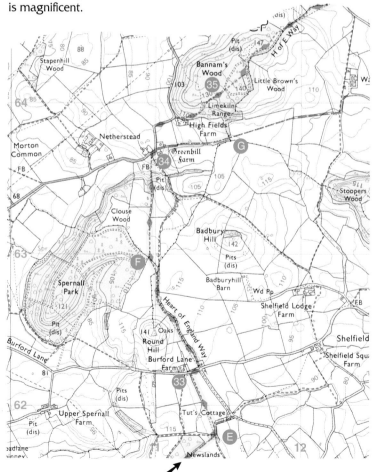

George House, Henley-in-Arden is sixteenth-century, though the façade is later.

Continue over a stile (or through the gap of an absent gate, despite the notice) and then through a gate. The path now descends past several splendid oak and ash trees, an echo of Bannam's Wood and the old Forest of Arden, to reach a stile on to a lane. Go through the hedge gap opposite and follow the hedge on the left, with a field on your right and pigs on the other side of the hedge. Go through a hedge gap and continue to a stile. Go over (or around!) to reach, after ten yards, a fine oak **H**. Now bear half-right across the field to the stile in the far hedge. Cross the next field to reach a bridge/stile, and maintain direction in the field beyond, going uphill to its top right-hand corner. Go over a stile and bear half-right to another stile. Cross and go half-left to the next stile, maintaining direction beyond it to descend to a wide green 'track' **I**. Here, go left over a narrow concrete bridge, and, after ten yards, cross a stile and go up steps to reach a stile and a helpful notice on how to reach the main road. The notice states that you should follow the tree line to a stile into the fenced paddock, then follow signs to a stile into an orchard, then go through the orchard to a drive and follow it to the road. The houses you pass, on the right, are Hunger Hill House and Well Cottage **36**.

Cross the road, with care, climb the stile opposite and go over the shallow ridge (keeping about 60 yards from the hedge on your left) to reach a partially concealed stile in the far hedge. Maintain direction to reach a bridge. Cross and follow the left-hand edge of the field beyond to reach a stile in the top corner. Cross this and follow a path enclosed by fences, passing allotments to the right to reach a fine, if unloved, Victorian passenger bridge, still in cream and brown, across the railway at Henley-in-Arden station. Cross the bridge and walk down to the road. Maintain direction across it and go up steps to reach a tarmac path, following it past houses to the left, and a road end on the right, to reach the car park of the White Swan Inn. Bear left and follow a short lane to the High Street of Henley-in-Arden **37**.

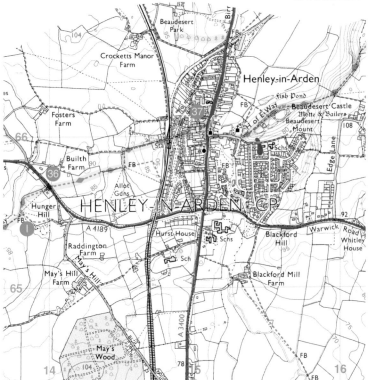

CIRCULAR WALK FROM ALCESTER

7 miles (11 km)

From the Town Hall, go back along the Heart of England Way (see page 78) along Malt Mill Lane, across the park, over the main road and along the road towards Oversley Green. Continue along the Way by turning right along Mill Lane and left along Primrose Lane. Cross the pedestrian bridge over the main road, but then leave the Way, bearing left down the hill. Go through a gate and follow the track uphill, going through a gate to reach Oversley Wood **31** a fine remnant of the Forest of Arden. Follow the track beside the wood, keeping it on your left, to reach a cross-tracks. Maintain direction, walking away from the wood with a hedge on your left. Cross a stile, then another over the fence on the right and walk uphill. Cross the ridge and descend to reach a stile on to Exhall cricket ground. Walk around the ground and along a drive to reach the road in the village. Exhall **38** is another of the villages mentioned in Shakespeare's verse com-

The restored Malt Mill Lane, Alcester, which now houses senior citizens.

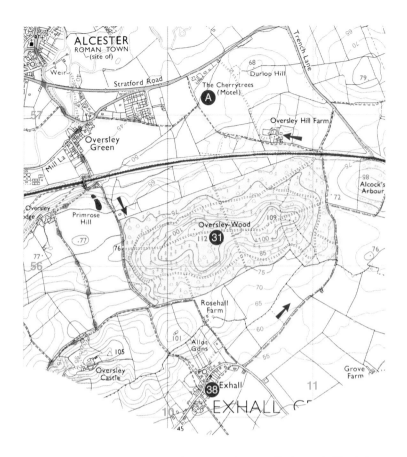

posed at Bidford (see page 72). Turn left to walk through 'Dodging Exhall'. A lane joins from the left near a right-hand bend: soon after, bear left along a signed track, following the hedge on the left to reach a gate. Go through and maintain direction, now with the hedge on your right. Go through a gate and follow the track beside Oversley Wood, with the wood on your left. Follow the track under the main road, then immediately turn left through a gate and follow the hedge on the right, passing Oversley Hill Farm, also on the right. Cross a stile and follow the hedge on the left, passing a pond and barn, on the left, to reach a gate. Go through and turn right (with a fence on the right) to reach a stile in the corner **A**. Do not cross the stile: instead, turn left to reach a gate. Follow the hedge on the left and cross a stile. Now bear half-right to reach a hedge corner. Cross the stile just beyond and follow a path, with houses on the right, to reach a road. Turn left to regain the Heart of England Way and follow it back into Alcester.

Circular walk from Henley-in-Arden

9 1/2 miles (15 km)

Go down the road beside St John's Church, as for the Heart of England Way, but where the road bears right (Alne Close), leave the Way, following the footpath ahead between the concrete fences to reach Meadow Road, to the right. Take this, following it to a T-junction. Turn right along Arden Road to reach the main road. Cross and go through the gate to the left of the cottages. Follow the hedge on the right and continue through the yard of Blackford Mill Farm **A**. The right of way now continues ahead. (If there are crops, go right in the yard, through a gate and follow a hedge on your right to the River Alne. Bear left and follow the river, rejoining the official right of way.) Follow the way across footbridges and over a field to reach Pettiford Lane, with Osier Bed Cottage to the left. Turn right, cross Pettiford Bridge **B** and, after a further 110 yards, turn left along a bridleway to reach the Stratford-upon-Avon Canal . Turn left and follow the canal towpath to reach the aqueduct over the main road **39**. Cross the aqueduct, then take the narrow path on the left that leads down to the main road (A3400), reaching it by the Navigation Inn, a reminder of the men who built the canal. As with all the other British 'navigations', the Stratford was dug by hand, the back-breaking work being performed by 'navigators' from which name the word 'navvie' for a labourer derives.

Follow the main road under the aqueduct and into Wootton Wawen **40**. The church here has Saxon origins and has some fine memorials, including an early fifteenth-century alabaster effigy of a knight and an early sixteenth-century tomb chest complete with brasses. To the east of the church is Wootton Hall, a fine seventeenth-century mansion which was once the home of Mrs Maria Fitzherbert, mistress (and later secret wife) of the Prince Regent (later George IV). The bridge over the River Alne (crossed on the entry to the village) includes a milestone stating 'London 100 miles'. It is said that when the Prince was in London he would often sigh and wish he was 100 miles away.

At the Bull Inn, bear left along the B4089 towards Alcester. Where the road bends sharp left **C** go ahead, under the railway bridge, and immediately turn right along Gorse Lane. At the far boundary of Gorse Cottage, on the right, turn right across a field to reach a footbridge. Follow the hedge on the left, cross into the next field and bear right to reach the railway. Cross, with care, and continue to reach Mayswood

Road. Turn left and follow the road towards Mary's Hill Farm. Just before the farm, turn right along a path following an old hedgeline. Maintain direction across the next two fields to reach Harper's Hill Farm. Bear right here, following the farm drive over a railway bridge, passing Ardenhurst School, on the right, to reach the main road (A3400). Turn left and follow the road back into Henley.

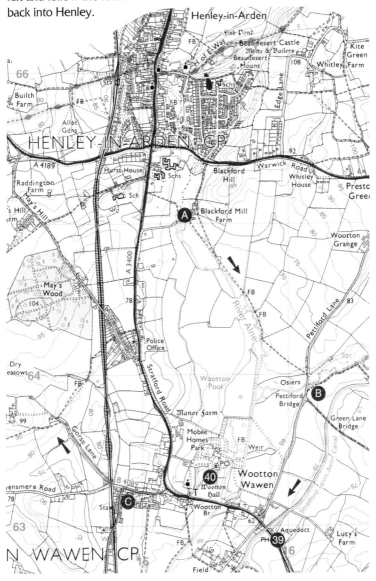

4 HENLEY-IN-ARDEN TO BERKSWELL

via Baddesley Clinton   *14 miles (22.4 km)*

Henley-in-Arden **37** is the link between Arden and Feldon, the Saxon forest and the open land, having grown up on Feldon Street, the old road which joined the edge of the forest to Warwickshire's pastoral landscape. By medieval times there were two villages here, the Norman de Montfort family having built a castle on the hillock to the east and called it Beaudesert because it was such a beautiful piece of uncultivated (i.e, waste) land. The castle seems never to have been more than small wood and stone structure, and was destroyed by the king after Peter de Montfort was killed (along with Simon de Montfort) at the battle of Evesham. Henley and Beaudesert survived the treason of their lord: Henley was granted a market charter and became prosperous, a prosperity which is reflected in the magnificent line of buildings in the High Street. Despite the fact that the High Street is also a main road, the view along it is one of the highlights of the Way. To the left from the White Swan, where the Way reaches the High Street, is the old Market Cross, one of few surviving in Warwickshire. It is fifteenth-century, but has not withstood the passage of time well, losing its four-sided head in 1894 and now having precautionary strap buttresses. Behind the Cross are the eighteenth-century Stone House, the delightful six-teenth-century George House (though much of the frontage is newer) and several old coaching inns from the same period. The White Swan is also a coaching inn, dating from the seventeenth century, though much restored. Opposite the White Swan is the Guildhall, built in 1448 by Ralph de Boteler and magnificently restored. The Guildhall is the home of the Court Leet, a medieval court that was concerned only with civil actions (and some minor offences) within the town, but which also ensured that local services ran smoothly. Today it has only symbolic powers, but still appoints a Butter Weigher, an Ale Taster and two Brook Lookers among other rather interesting positions. Beside the Guildhall is the Church of St John the Baptist, a fine fif-teenth-century building in the Perpendicular style.

From the car park of the White Swan, turn right along the High Street, then left, passing between St John's Church and Barclays Bank, to follow Beaudesert Lane past St Nicholas's Church, which is older than the town church, having been built by the de Montforts in about 1170. Where the lane bends sharp right into Alne Close, go through the kissing gate at the end of the pavement on the left beside the churchyard and follow the path uphill across the mound once occupied by Beaudesert Castle.

Maintain direction across a second peak, descend and then ascend again, heading towards a telegraph pole on the horizon and ignoring paths to both left and right. Cross a stile and follow the fence/hedge on the right. Cross a stile on the right and follow a faint path diagonally across the field beyond to reach a stile in the thick hedge opposite. Turn sharp left along an enclosed path to reach a waymarker. Here, turn right, going through a gateless gap and across a field, aiming for the mid-point of two trees to reach the lane leading to Hungerfield Farm on the left.

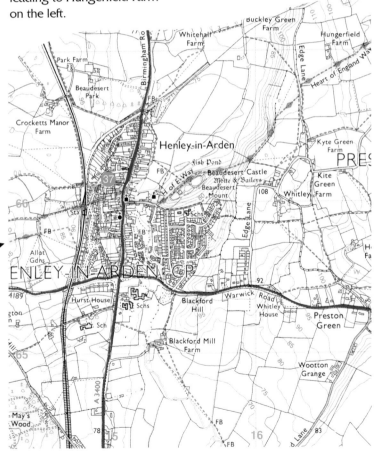

Go through a gap and maintain direction across a field to reach another hedge gap. Follow the hedge on the left until it turns left, then bear half-left to reach a stile in the field corner, crossing it into a small copse. Go through the copse and cross the field beyond, aiming for a point between two trees in the far hedge. Cross a stile and follow the hedge on the right at first, then bear left towards the conifers to the right of Holly Bank Farm. Cross a stile and pass the farm's garden to reach another stile. Beyond this, follow the hedge on the right, then bear left to reach the farm drive, following it to a road.

Turn left on the road and follow it around a right-hand bend, and then turn left along a drive for 'Bushwood, Coppice Corner'. Cross a disused railway line, then turn right through a gate and cross a field towards a telegraph pole, going through the smaller of two gates and turning right to reach a stile. The path beyond follows conifer woodland on the left and runs parallel to the old railway, about 60 yards off to the right, and leads you to a waymarker which directs you into the wood. Bear right and walk through the wood to reach a stile. Cross into a field, following the edge of the wood on the right to the field corner. Cross two stiles, turning right to continue between a hedge and the wood. After 60 yards and just beyond a bridge over the old railway, go over a stile on the left and across the field beyond, heading towards the red-brick house to reach a stile on to a lane.

Turn left into the lane, passing the house (a nice old house with lovely honeysuckle) and follow it to a crossroads in

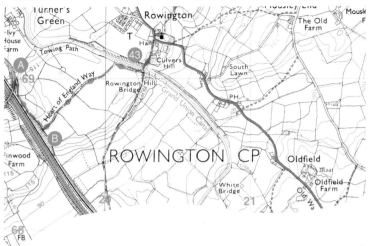

Lowsonford **41** with a telephone box on the right and the old village pump ahead on the left. Go straight ahead, following the road to the Stratford-upon-Avon Canal **42**. The canal was begun in 1802, though it was to be fourteen years before the 25-mile (40 km) waterway had linked the Warwickshire and Birmingham Canal at King's Norton to the Avon at Stratford. There are 56 locks along the route, one of which lies just to the west of the road bridge which takes the Way to the other bank.

Cross the canal and continue along the road for a further mile (1.6 km) to cross the M40 motorway. Once over the motorway **A** immediately turn right along a concrete track, going through a gate. Follow the track to a Cellnet station **B**. Here, turn sharp left along a rough track, with a hedge on your left and a field to your right, and follow the track, which bears right as you near the canal, until you reach a lane. Turn left along the lane to reach the Grand Union Canal **43**. The canal, which links the Thames at Brentford to Birmingham, runs for a distance of 135 miles (215 km) and has 165 locks. The most spectacular of the locks are the flight at Hatton, a little way east of the Way, where 21 locks raise (or lower) barges almost 146½ ft (45m). Closer to the Way, at Shrewley, there is a very interesting feature where the towpaths of the canal go through their own tunnels above a canal tunnel. The angled towpath tunnels allowed the horses to leave the barges and return to them later, while the bargees propelled the barges through the canal tunnel by lying on their backs and 'walking' along the tunnel roof. Closer to the Way is one of the most pleasant sections of the canal, which runs between embankments through some beautiful countryside.

Cross the canal and pass a house on the right to reach a T-junction in Rowington **44**. Turn left, then immediately right into the churchyard. St Lawrence's Church is Norman in origin, but has been much altered and restored. Follow the gravel track to the left of the church, bearing left with it to pass a curious building. Go down steps, cross a stile, and follow the fence on the left to another stile. Cross and turn right, following the hedge on the right to a stile by a gate. Cross and continue beside the hedge until it turns sharp right. From here continue straight on past the trees ahead to reach a stile and, maintaining direction, go downhill to pass through a gate. Follow the hedge on the left until it goes sharp left, then bear half-left, staying about 35 yards to the left of a farm to reach a stile. Maintain direction, leaving a house elegantly constructed around an old windmill on the left, to reach a gate on to a road.

Claimed to the most perfect example of a medieval manor house in England, Baddesley Clinton Manor is also unusual in being surrounded by a moat.

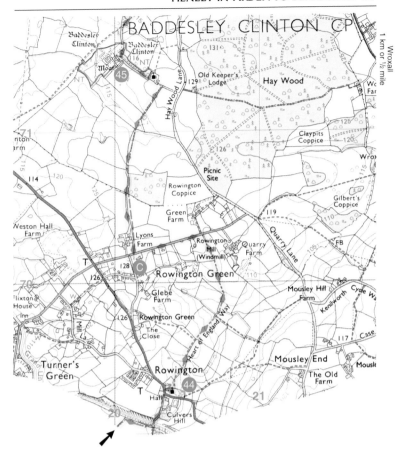

Turn left for 550 yards (500m), then turn right **C** through a gate and follow the rough track past Lyons Farm and a large hay barn, on the left. Follow the track through a gate, then, where it turns sharp left, go through the gate ahead, following the hedge on the left. Go through a gate, over a concrete track and through another gate to reach a path running between a fence and a hedge. Baddesley Clinton Church is now glimpsed through the trees ahead. Step right, then turn sharp left through a gate. Go through a kissing gate into the churchyard and pass to the left of the church to reach a gate. Follow the very pleasant path beyond to reach a drive, with Baddesley Clinton Manor **45** to the left.

The Manor House at Baddesley Clinton is claimed by many to be the perfect example of a late medieval manor. The Clintons of the name were the first to construct a mansion here, digging the moat as protection, though the present house was built by the Bromes, who had bought the manor in the late fifteenth century. With its bridge across the moat, its creeper-clad walls and perfect lines and dimensions, the house is achingly picturesque. Inside there is a fine collection of seventeenth- and eighteenth-century furniture and some interesting paintings. It is, however, the exterior that holds the eye: follow the moat around the house, a journey upon which you will be accompanied by several flocks of ducks who have long ago worked out that visitors mean food, for the very best short walk on the Way. The Manor complex also has a restaurant/coffee house, though it is necessary to pay the National Trust's entrance fee (and, of course, to find the site open) to reach it. St Michael's Church, beside the Manor House, is a neat building, another construction of the Brome family. One member, Nicholas Brome, who died in 1517, has an extraordinary grave. Nicholas's father, John Brome, had been murdered in 1468 by John Herthill (a steward to 'Warwick the Kingmaker', Richard Neville of Warwick Castle) in a dispute over land. Nicholas was a violent man: in 1471 he avenged his father by killing Herthill, then in 1483 he killed again. The record of the crime states that he 'slew ye minister of Baddesley Church findinge him in his plor [parlour] chockinge his wife under ye chinne.' Whether the 'chucking' under the chin was an innocent gesture or an indication of something deeper is not recorded. Nicholas, overcome by guilt at the murder of a minister, built a steeple on Packwood Church and gave instructions that he be buried inside the door of Baddesley Church so that everyone would walk over his grave, seeing this as a fitting penance.

Turn right, passing the Manor House car park on the right. There is another drive running parallel on the left: where the two drives meet, bear right through a kissing gate and follow the enclosed path beyond through very pleasant woodland. Cross a stile and a bridge. Beyond, the path (still enclosed) is overgrown with ferocious nettles: battle across three stiles to reach a road and turn left to reach a T-junction. Turn right for about 20 yards, then go left along the drive of the smartly-gated Convent Farm. The Poor Clares' convent is a little further along the road.

At the end of the drive there is a roundabout involving two bridges **D,** an elaborate part of the access to the house on the right: go through the wooden gate and cross the yard to another gate. Cross a small field to a metal gate, and continue along the hedge on the right, passing through an empty gateway and going over a stile. When a hedge joins from the left, cross a stile and follow the hedge

on the left to reach a stile/gate on to a road at Chadwick End **46**. Go
left for 10 yards (the Orange Tree Inn is just ahead) then cross and
take the drive opposite to reach the end of a cul-de-sac street **E**. Bear
right across the street to reach a tarmac square, with garages on the
left. Go behind the last garage, following a narrow path, with garden
fences to the left, to reach a stile. Cross and follow the hedge on the
right to the field corner, maintaining direction through a pleasant
copse. At the end of the copse, cross a wide, mucky track to reach a
stile. Go diagonally across the field beyond to reach a redundant stile
on to a tractor track. Turn left and follow the track through a gateway
and continue on to cross a stiled bridge. Continue, with a fence on
the right, across three stiles. Beyond the third, bear half-left across a
field, heading towards the houses on Oldwich Lane East. Cross a
stile into a field with large clumps of celandine, maintaining direction
to reach a boardwalk across a marshy section. Cross a stiled bridge
and continue ahead across two fields, connected by a stile, to reach
a stile in a thick hedge. Cross on to
Oldwich Lane **F**.

1 km or ½ mile
Wroxall

Turn right for 20 yards, then go left along a short section of scruffy path to a stile. Follow the fence on the left, then, where it turns sharp left, maintain direction to reach a stile. Cross and turn left so as to maintain direction, with a hedge on your left. Cross two stiles, the second made redundant by a neighbouring gap, and continue to the field end. Turn left over a triple-decker stile and follow the hedge on the right for about 20 yards to reach a superb oak tree. Oldwich House Farm can be seen over on the left. Cross the stile on the right and follow the hedge on the right to a thicket. Go through this into a field. Follow the hedge/bank on the left and, where it ends, maintain direction across two fields to reach a rough track. Follow this to the drive to Balsall Lodge Farm on the left. Go ahead along the drive to reach a road. To the left from here is Temple Balsall **47,** named for the Knights Templar who owned it in the thirteenth century. In the churchyard is the grave of Henry Williams who wrote the music for 'It's a long way to Tipperary'. Williams was an entertainer and the words were written by a colleague of his, Jack Judge. The song was first performed by the pair in 1912 at the Plough Inn at Meer End **48** which was owned by Williams' uncle. Originally it was a long way to Connemara, but later in the same year Judge accepted a bet to write and perform a new song at the Grand Theatre in Stalybridge, Cheshire within 24 hours. It seems he changed the destination to Tipperary in order to salve his conscience! The Plough at Meer End is now called the Tipperary Inn.

Turn right for 20 yards, then go left along a narrow lane with a high wooden fence on the left. Cross a field close to its right-hand edge, go over a broken stile and continue with a hedge on the right, crossing a further stile. At the end of the next field **G** there are stiles ahead and on the right: go over the one on the right and follow the hedge on the right towards a pylon. Cross a stile and maintain direction, passing a remnant section of hedge on the right. Go past a redundant stile and continue to another stile and a footbridge. Now head for the corner of the hedge coming towards the top of the field ahead and to the right of the tall trees in front of the buildings on the right. Walk with the hedge on your left to reach a stile on to a road, Magpie Lane. To the right from here is Magpie Farm **49** a superb sixteenth-century timber-framed house.

Turn left, passing Balsall Farm House, a fine late seventeenth-century house, to reach a long, low, green barn. Here, turn right through the hedge to reach a stile. Follow the hedge on the right to a waymarker post and bear half-left there, passing a fine 'black and brick' house on the right (there is considerable rebuilding

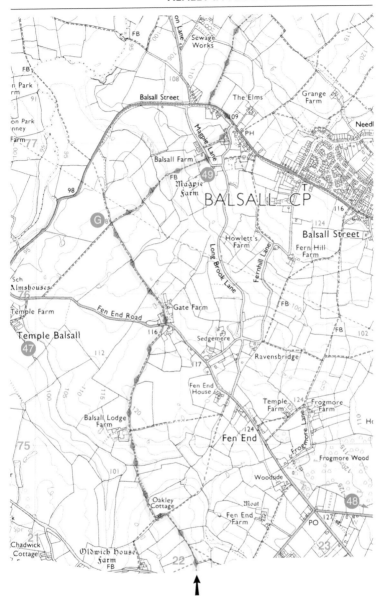

going on here: note, too, the black and white Wendy house!) and head for a white house (Jessamine Cottage) with a delightful turret. Cross a stile on to a lane and turn left, passing the cottage, to reach a T-junction. Ye Olde Saracen's Head Inn is a few yards to the right.

Turn left along the road for 220 yards (200m), then turn right over a stile beside a gate and follow the hedge on the left over two stiles.

Berkswell Church has the best crypt of any parish church in England.

Maintain direction across a field, crossing a footbridge in the middle to reach a stile in the far hedge. Bear right, then left to walk with a hedge on your right. Bear right to cross a stile and follow the hedge on the left over two stiles and a footbridge to reach the right-hand corner of a wood. Go through a gate on to a drive and bear right along it. Go through the gateposts of Wootton Grange **50** (the house is to your left as you join the drive) and continue along the lane to a T-junction. Go right and you will come to a T-junction with the A452 dual carriageway.

Go left beside the main road for 275 yards (250m), then cross, with extreme care, and take the road for Berkswell, following it for 330 yards (300m) to reach a kissing gate on the left. Follow a path between hedges/fences, then along the left edge of a field, to reach a track. Bear right with the track, but soon step right through a kissing gate with the lake of Berkswell Hall to the left and follow a path over a footbridge and across duckboards. Berkswell Church **51** is now visible ahead. Cross a stile at the end of the duckboards and follow the fence to the left, with Berkswell Hall now visible on the left, to reach a stile into the churchyard.

Berkswell is the best Norman church in Warwickshire, with a complete nave and chancel and a crypt, one of very few survivals of the period and most certainly the best crypt of any parish church in Britain. In the crypt – reached by damp steps: there is a light switch ahead as you go through the small 'gate' – there are some small remnants of original medieval wall paintings. The crypt, delicately vaulted and softly orange when the lights are lit, is a very beautiful place. The western part of it is octagonal, a unique feature: it is speculated that the shape derives from an earlier Saxon crypt, the present crypt dating from the mid-twelfth century. Almost as good as the crypt is the church porch, a marvellous sixteenth-century timber-framed building, constructed as the priest's house, but then used as the village school and council room. It is now the vestry. Close to the porch is the grave of a local youth who died of a broken heart at the age of twenty when, as the inscription notes he was 'Deceived by one I lov'd, I lov'd most dear'. The well of the village name is the huge (16 feet / 5m square) stone tank to the right beyond the church gate. It is not clear what its original purpose was, though some have speculated that it was for immersion baptisms which, if true, cannot have been much fun in cold weather. Today it contains no water, despite the notice implying dire consequences for those who bathe their dogs. In the village beyond the well there is a pleasant little green with the old village stocks still in place.

Follow the gravel path leaving the church to your left to reach a gate. Go through with the well to your right and after 6 yards turn left through a kissing gate and follow the edge of the churchyard to another kissing gate. After a further 12 yards, go through another kissing gate, then follow the hedge on the right to reach a stile. Walk 20 yards along the enclosed path to reach a kissing gate on to a road.

5 BERKSWELL TO KINGSBURY

via Meriden and Shustoke   *15 miles (24 km)*

Having walked through the churchyard at Berkswell and followed the path beyond, the wayfarer has arrived at a road. Turn left for 330 yards (300m), then go right up the track towards Blind Hall Farm. Cross a cattle grid and pass the farm on your left, continuing uphill to another cattle grid. Beyond this, go left and then right over two stiles and turn left to follow the hedge on the left around to the right to reach another stile. Continue with the hedge on your left, crossing a stile and going through a hedge gap. When the hedge on the left ends, maintain direction to join a hedge on the right, following it to a stile/gate on to a road opposite a house called The Byre **52**.

The porch of Berkswell church was built in the sixteenth century as the priest's house. It was later the village school, before becoming the vestry.

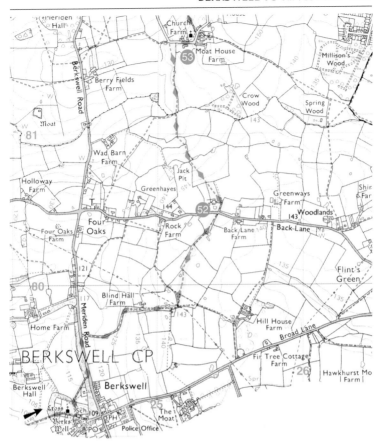

Cross the road and follow the drive towards The Byre. Go over the stile ahead and follow the fence on the right to another stile. Cross and bear half-left across a field to a gate/stile. Follow a faint path 5 yards from the hedge on the right to reach a stile by a gate. Bear half-left to another stile in the far hedge, then follow the hedge on the right to yet another stile. Bear right along the field's right-hand edge (with a huge farm off to the left) to reach a waymarker post. Here, bear left across the field to reach a gate on to a lane. Turn right to reach St Lawrence's Church **53**.

The original village in this northern part of the Forest of Arden was founded by the Saxons and called Alspath, a name that lives on in Alspath House which is passed further along the way. Alspath is famed as the birthplace of Lady Godiva. Although her famous naked ride is almost certainly a myth, Godiva was actually a real person

By tradition, the ancient village cross on the green at Meriden marks the centre (the Heart) of England, though the Way passes a little way to the east.

and is credited with having founded the first church on the site of the present St Lawrence's. Nothing of that original Saxon church now remains (though it is known that it was dedicated to the Saxon St Edmund), even the Norman building which replaced it having been rebuilt, though the present chancel is from the first Norman work, raised, legend has it, by a Norman knight called Ivo in penance for some unrecorded, but clearly dreadful, crime. Inside there are two interesting effigies of knights, one in alabaster from the fifteenth century; the other, in stone, perhaps half a century later.

Follow the road past the church on the left and the magnificent 'black and brick' fifteenth-century Moat House Farm on the right (a real reminder that this is Shakespeare Country). Ahead now is a fine white house, known as Dr Kittermaster's House. Dr James Kittermaster, who died in 1876, was a surgeon, but also a notable water colourist, his works giving a vivid indication of how the area around Meriden looked in the middle of the nineteenth century. Further along the road, past the house on the right, is Alspath House.

Just before Dr Kittermaster's House, turn left through a gate into the churchyard. Dr Kittermaster's grave is just to the left. Bear right, passing, on the right, the grave of Dr Edward and Christiana Clarke. Christiana was the sister of Mary Ann Evans, the real name of the novelist George Eliot, who is known to have visited the village on many occasions. The sisters were born at South Farm, Arbury, about 5 miles (8km) to the east of the Way when it reaches Green End. Dr and Mrs Clarke lived in the Bull's Head before the building (which had been a coaching inn called the Red Lion some years earlier) re-opened as an inn.

Continue through the churchyard to reach a kissing gate and then follow the hedge on the right to another. Continue, with a severe fence on the right and with noise audible from the main road ahead. Meriden village is visible over on the left. When the severe fence turns sharp right, maintain direction along an old iron fence with hawthorn trees. Go through two kissing gates within about 15 yards of each other to reach the main road. Cross with care and go down steps into the car park of the Queen's Head Inn **54**. The inn has been licensed for over 300 years and is still popular despite its being a little way out of the 'new' village of Meriden **55**. It seems appropriate, in view of the name of Way, to make a pilgrimage into the village. Here, at the western end of the village green, stands a cross with a tapering octagonal shaft which, tradition has it, marks

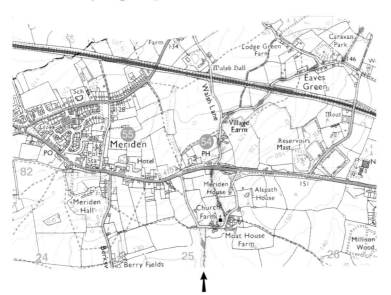

the centre of England. The claim has been disputed, and the cross (an old market cross) has been moved several times, but the tradition holds, and Meriden is certainly the best-known of several 'centres'. At the other end of the green from the cross is the Cyclists' Memorial raised in 1921 in memory of cyclists who had died in the 1914-18 War, but now dedicated to those who died in both World Wars. Meriden had (and still has) a history of popularity among cyclists and was seen as the most appropriate place for the memorial. The memorial is the focus of a cyclists' rally each May. Enthusiasts of two-wheelers of a quicker sort will want to visit the Meriden Hotel where the Triumph bar commemorates the Triumph motor-cycle factory that once made Meriden famous throughout the world. The factory is long gone, its site engulfed by a housing estate, but just a short distance to the west the National Motorcycle Museum provides an opportunity to pay homage to that aspect of the area's history. Also to the west, just a few hundred yards away, is Forest Hall, the headquarters of the Woodmen of Arden, a famous company of archers who carry on the archery tradition established by hunters in the forest. The Hall was built in 1788 by Joseph Bonomi, an Italian architect.

From the inn car park **A** follow the road heading northwards on the right-hand side of the inn car park (marked 'Except for Access') *not* the road heading east (which is a slip road for the main road). Follow the road past a junction on the left and then under the main A45 to reach an angled T-junction. Bear right (signed 'Coventry 5$\frac{1}{4}$'), passing Eaves Green Park Homes Estate and a drive to a house on the left. Turn left **B** after a further 33 yards, crossing a stile set back from the road. Follow the hedge on the right, crossing another stile and the Meriden Riding School field, before going through a hedge gap into a second field. Head towards the bottom left-hand field corner (passing a waymarker post), where you cross a footbridge and a stile into woodland. The wood is called Meriden Shafts and is another remnant of the old Forest of Arden. Meriden derives from the old word for a cherry tree and there may still be a few in the old copses. It would be fun to discover that Shafts derives from arrows, appropriate enough in a wood close to the headquarters of the Woodmen of Arden, but it actually derives from old mines which, despite the name, were 'open cast' – more pits than shafts.

Follow the path through the wood, soon reaching a fence on the left. When the fence goes sharp left, maintain direction to exit the wood over a stile. Turn left for about 50 yards to reach a stile in the hedge on the right. Cross this and follow the hedge on the right,

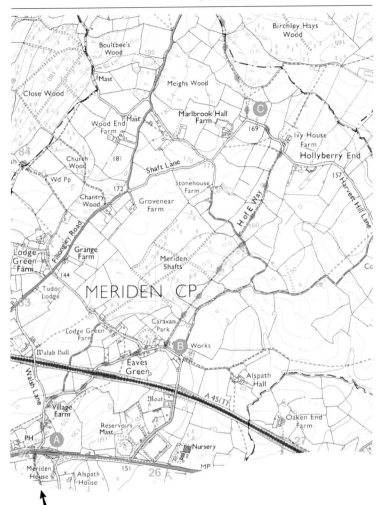

going through two hedge gaps (the second in a neatly trimmed privet hedge!) to reach a stile on to a road. To the left here is the unsupported gable end of an old house ('Gable end seeks other walls and roof with a view to becoming a house'!?), while Ivy House Farm is just ahead.

Turn left along the road for **440 yards (400m)** (ignoring the first path on the right) to reach a sharp left-hand bend **C**. Here there is a waymarker post and a road sign for Harvest Hill. Turn right over a footbridge/stile and cross a meadow to a double stile. Maintain direction across a field to reach a waymarker in the facing hedge. Turn left and follow the woodland edge on your right, and then a field edge on the left, going around the field corner to reach a stile on the left leading on to a road opposite Hayes Hill Farm. Turn left, passing, to the left of the farm which has a lake with what appears to be a diving board. Go through a gate on the right at the end of the farmyard **D** and cross a field to a stile beside gate. Follow the hedge on the right with the noise of the M6 motorway ahead, then, where the field edge bears left, go right towards a prominent dead tree to reach a stile. Go half-right to another stile at the bottom right-hand corner of the next field, cross and follow the hedge, later a fence, on the right to reach a stile leading on to a farm bridge over the motorway **56**. Cross the stile beside the gate ahead and stay to the left of the hawthorn trees to reach a gate/stile.

Maintain direction towards Barrat's Farm, going to the right of the barn to reach a stile. Follow a section of shuttered path to reach a stile on to a lane. Turn left, and then right over a stile. Head for the houses on the left ahead to reach a stile by a gate and cattle trough. Now head for the left side of the houses to reach a stile on to a road. Bear right, passing 'Cornerways' at Green End **57** to reach a T-junction. Bear right across the road, go over a stile and follow a track with a hedge on the right to reach a house. Here the track stops: go to the left of the row of trees bordering the house and cross a stile. Go right, then follow the field edge round to the left to reach a stile on to a road. Cross to the stile opposite and walk ahead across a field to reach a stile in the far hedge. Bear half-right to the far corner of the field beyond and cross a stile on the right. Follow the hedge on the left to reach a stile and cross this, followed by a footbridge and another stile. Now head across a field towards a prominent tree at a hedge corner. Follow the hedge on your right, go through a hedge gap and cross the field beyond towards the trees to reach a stile on to a road **58**.

Turn left, passing the drive to High House and Hardingwood Lane, both on the left. Go past Colliers Oak Farm on the right and, after a further 330 yards (300m), turn right over a stile. Bear half-left to the point where an intermittent hedge reaches the edge of Parsons Wood.

Bear left, with the wood on the right, to reach a stile into a field **E**. This is a huge field, and at the time of writing the right-of-way, which bears slightly left to the bottom left-hand corner, was obscured by a wheat crop. If that is the case, turn left and follow the hedge on the left around to the far corner where a gap in the hedge leads to a road. Turn left for a few yards to reach a T-junction. Turn right along the only unsigned road. Now, about 10 yards before the next T-junction, turn left past a redundant stile and cross a sleeper bridge. Follow a path

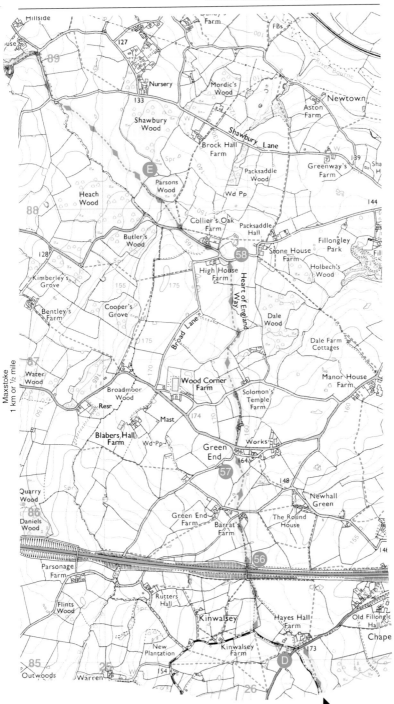

through the very pleasant Dumble Wood **59**. The wood, with some good oaks, also once had a fine crop of hazel which was coppiced for fencing and sheep hurdles, but the practice was stopped sometime ago. Now the undergrowth is impenetrable, suggesting that, once nature has been given a hand, the hand needs to be permanently offered or it will be many years before order is re-established.

Cross a stile and follow the right-hand edge of a long field to reach another stile. Cross and immediately turn right over a stile to regain the wood which has narrowed to a mere ribbon at this point. Go down steps, cross a footbridge and go up steps into a field. Maintain direction, heading for a prominent tree with a pylon behind it and bear left there to reach a fine oak tree standing on what was once clearly the hedgeline between fields. Step down into the next field and turn right, following the hedge on the right until it turns sharp right **F**. A sign here claims the right of way has been diverted, but the suggested line is as on the map, turning half-left and aiming for the red-brick building to the left of the nearest power pylon. However, here too, at the time of writing, the right-of-way was obscured (by a potato crop), requiring a long detour around the field edge. Either way you will reach the hedge in front of the red building. Walk with this hedge on your right to reach a track. Cross the track to The Metlins Farm which is on the right, and follow the hedge on the right to a stiled bridge. The next stile is 10 yards in from the hedge on the right: cross this, and the field beyond, heading for the spire of the church at Church End **60**. Go past two fine oak trees, cross a stile and follow the hedge on the right to reach a lane by means of a gap in the hedge.

Go ahead for about 65 yards to reach a right-hand bend. Here, cross a stile on the left and follow the hedge on the right, still heading for the church spire as you cross another stile, and, at the end of the next field, a footbridge and stile. At the end of the next field, cross a stile and turn sharp left along a diverted path **G**. Follow the hedge on the left, crossing a stile and continuing to the bottom corner of the next field. Here, turn right, still with the hedge on your left, and cross three stiles, the last one leading on to Church Road beside a little group of pretty cottages, mid-way between Shustoke to the left and Church End to the right. Church End is so-called because the parish church stands there. St Cuthbert's is an early fourteenth-century church, built of red sandstone and with the spire that has served as a landmark over the last few fields. Inside there is an understated memorial to Sir William Dugdale, seventeenth-century owner of Blyth Hall, a fine house standing of the western side of Shustoke village.

Cross the road and a stile and follow the hedge on the left, with the spire of St Cuthbert's church now dominating the horizon on the right. Cross a stile in the bottom left-hand corner of the field and continue to follow the hedge on the left, turning right, left and right with it. Now turn left over a stile and cross two footbridges to reach the Shustoke Reservoirs **61**. These were created to provide water to Birmingham, but after the construction of the Elan Valley reservoirs in mid-Wales

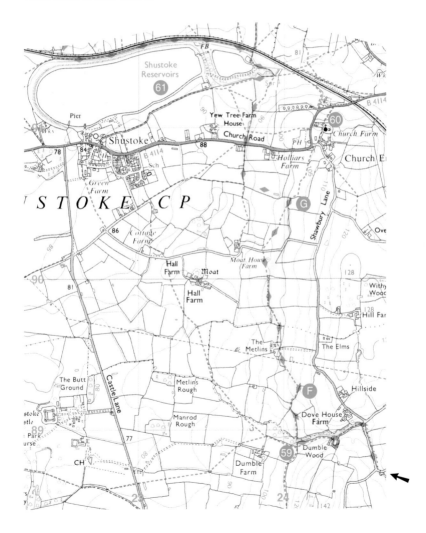

they were used to supply Nuneaton and Coventry. There is a gate to the left here. Do not go through: instead follow a path through a pretty avenue, passing a building on the left then going between the reservoir on the left and Water Board machinery on the right, crossing a footbridge to reach a railway line. Go through a gate on the left and follow a path beside the railway. Ignore two stiles on the right which give access to paths crossing the railway and pass a signal to reach another stile on the right, just before a brick bridge over the railway **H**. Cross the railway here, with care, and follow the hedge on the left until it bears off to the left. Now maintain direction, heading to the left of a house. Bear left beside the house fence, which is hung with beautiful honeysuckle, to reach a stile. Cross to reach a road at a junction. Go straight over, cross a stile and go diagonally (half-left from the road) to reach another stile. Follow the hedge on the left and, where it ends, maintain direction along the old boundary between two fields to reach a waymarker in the next hedge **I**. Here, ignore the sleeper bridge on the left and turn right and then almost immediately left over two stiles, crossing a ditch. Walk parallel to the hedge 10 yards on your right, cross a footbridge and follow the hedge on the right to reach a delightful footbridge over the railway. Do not cross: instead, go through the gate to its right and follow the path beside the railway, eventually bearing right past houses to reach a road.

Turn right along the road to reach a turning on the right for Hoggrill's End. Here, turn left over a stile and bear half-right across a small field to reach a stile. Go diagonally across the next field to a stile in the far hedge. Now head to the right of the large tree and continue on to reach a stile on to a road opposite a 'No Through Road' sign. Cross and follow this road, passing several attractive houses. Where the road curves away to the left, continue along the signed bridleway ahead, going through a gate and continuing through an avenue of trees to reach a gate into a field. There are two tractor tracks ahead: take the left-hand one, going diagonally across the field, aiming well to the right of a barn. At the far side of the field follow the more established tractor track gently uphill to reach a road at a T-junction in Foul End.

Go straight ahead along the road signed for Hurley. Then, at a waymarker just before the houses on the left **J,** cross a footbridge hidden in undergrowth on the left and follow the hedge on the left, walking a delicate course between fearsome nettles and the crop on the right. Maintain direction to reach a waymarker and turn right there, crossing the field to reach a hedge corner. Continue, with a hedge on your

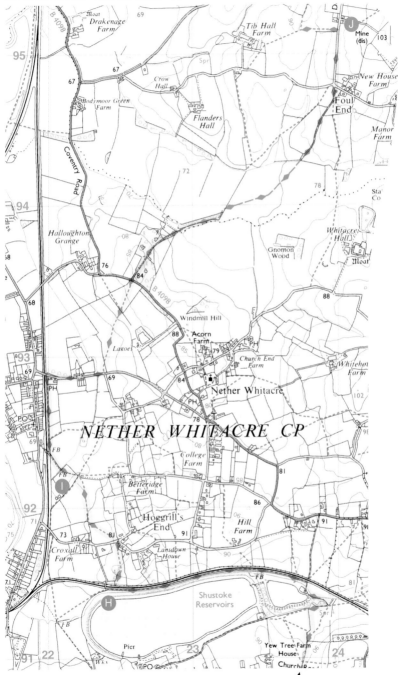

left, to reach a stile in the corner of the field. Continue beside the hedge on the left, crossing a footbridge/stile and maintaining direction to reach a stile on to a road. To the right is the Post Office and General Store in Hurley **62**. Hurley Hall, at the far end of the village from where the Way enters, is a fine early Georgian house.

Turn left, then first right up a road to reach a very sharp left-hand bend. Go through the gate ahead and follow the hedge on the right (with the tower of Kingsbury Church ahead) to reach an oak tree where the hedge ends. Now bear half-left across the field ahead, heading to the left of the church tower. Do not be deterred if you hear gunfire ahead – when you top the ridge you will see targets to the right and a wooded firing range ahead: aim for the extreme left edge of the woodland to reach the range boundary. There, turn left along the perimeter, turning right at a range flagpole. The next flagpole is at a road and barrier: cross the road and follow the wide grass track, bearing right with it, and then left to reach the main road. Cross, with care, and follow the hedge on the right past good oak and ash trees, with some less attractive grey, squat storage tanks further to the right. Go up steps, cross the railway with care and descend steps to a stile. Follow the enclosed path with houses to the left. Now, where the path goes left **K**, go ahead for 5 yards, then down steps on the right. Turn left, with a hedge/fence on the left, cross a footbridge and bear right at a path fork, following a gravel track to the road in Kingsbury.

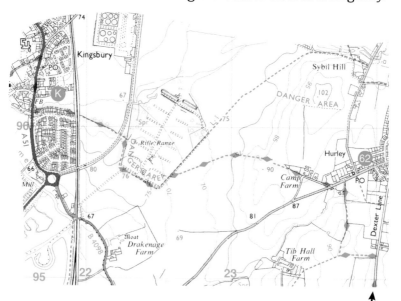

The spire of St Cuthbert's at Church End acts as a waymarker for walkers approaching Shustoke. Here it seen beyond one of the Shustoke reservoirs.

6 KINGSBURY TO LICHFIELD

via Drayton Bassett   *14 miles (22.4 km)*

Having reached the main road in Kingsbury, cross, with care, and turn right, passing the Royal Oak Inn on the left. Then, just before the White Swan Inn, turn left, following the road past a bus shelter on the left.

Turn left along a track with a metal fence on the left. Where the track bears right, step to the left to reach a waymarker and follow a path at the edge of the churchyard. The church of St Peter and St Paul **63** is largely Norman, though the tower is later. Unfortunately, due to theft and vandalism, the church is rarely open, depriving many visitors of seeing some interesting items. If you do gain entry, look out for the fine, twelve-sided font on a hexagonal base and the fourteenth-century wall painting above the east window. The church also has 'Green Men', their faces sprouting oak leaves from the mouth. Though relatively rare, pagan heads are seen surprisingly often in churches: Kingsbury has two, one high in the roof to the left of the entrance door, the other as a corbel supporting the arch between the north aisle and the Bracebridge Chapel. The other end of the arch has a grotesque as a corbel. To the right of the church is Kingsbury Hall, originally built in the fourteenth century by the Bracebridge family for whom the chapel in the church is named, but subsequently added to and modified. The original building was fortified, in part by the natural defence afforded by the steep cliff above the River Tame.

Descend steep steps and continue to a footbridge over the river **A**, crossing it to reach Kingsbury Water Park **64**. The Water Park covers 600 acres and includes 30 lakes, created by the filling of pits from which gravel has been extracted over the last 50 years. The park is, in part, the result of allowing nature to reclaim the land, and in part the product of landscaping carried out with the aim of creating specific habitats in order to increase the diversity of species – this has been highly successful, despite the intense leisure use of the Park, especially with birds and water insects such as dragonflies. Bird species seen regularly include all the British terns except for the Sandwich tern. There is also a breeding colony of common terns. Reed buntings and grasshopper warblers nest among the reeds, little ringed plovers, water rails and Temminck's stint have been seen in the lakes margins and there are kingfishers on the river. Osprey, marsh harrier, hen harrier and hobby are the rarer of the birds of prey that have visited the Park. A leaflet obtainable from the Visitor Centre, just a few yards south of the Way, describes a short nature trail around some of the lake, with information on the history of the pools and the trees and birds which may be seen. There is also a coffee shop at the Visitor Centre.

After crossing the bridge, turn right and head for a pylon, crossing, or going around, a football pitch. Go past a waymarker post and a track on the left (still heading for the pylon) to reach another waymarker and another track from the left at an adventure playground. Take the track on the left to another waymarker and turn sharp right there to go along a gravel track, passing a lake with lovely water lilies on the right. Ignore a track on the left (signed for the Visitor Centre) and continue ahead following the sign for the Broomey Croft car park and going under the M42. At the next track junction turn right (signed for the Broomey Croft Rare Breeds Farm and Granary Tea Rooms), then turn left at the next junction to reach the Broomey Croft car park. Go straight through the car park, with Broomey Croft Pool on your right. At the corner of the pool, go through a small wooded area and turn right along a gravel track, following it to reach the towpath of the Birmingham and Fazeley Canal **65**. The canal links

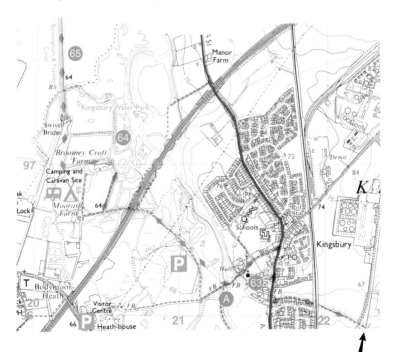

Farmer's Bridge Junction, Birmingham with Fazeley a little to the north, near Tamworth, from where the continuation to Coventry was known as the Coventry Canal. This name change was the result of convoluted ownership and trading disputes which led to legal battles between the various Midland canal owners at the end of the eighteenth century when the canal was being dug. The Birmingham and Fazeley, along with all the other canals of the BCN (the Birmingham Canal Navigations), has its bridges named rather than numbered. The Drayton Foot Bridge is unique in having spiral stairways within its supporting towers and a Gothic-like span. It is said that this design was adopted at the insistence of the Peel family of Drayton Park.

Follow the towpath, passing several bridges, to reach the Drayton Foot Bridge with the Drayton Swivel Bridge just beyond. Cross the footbridge to reach the main road. Cross it, bearing slightly to the left, with care, and take the road to Drayton Bassett. This road passes some lovely houses, but should be followed with great care as, apart from the first few yards where there is a pavement on the right, there is no verge. Follow the road to the village green **66**.

Drayton Manor, to the north of the village, was bought by Robert Peel in 1790. Robert became Sir Robert, as did his son who became Prime Minister, and is famed for having established the Metropolitan Police force (and giving his name to the first constables, who were known as 'peelers'). The second Sir Robert was a somewhat cheerless

The Way crosses Drayton Foot Bridge, using spiral stairs in the twin towers.

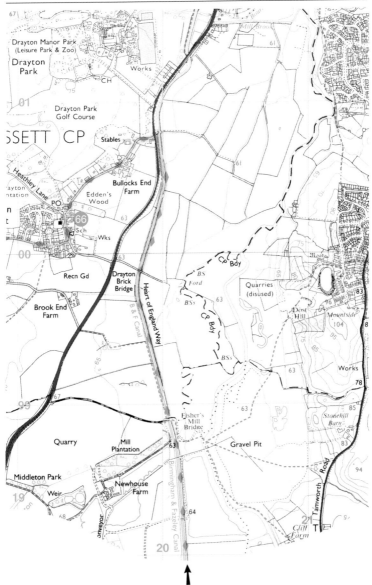

landlord, refusing permission for the opening of a village inn: there is still no pub in Drayton Bassett, though the Working Men's Club opposite the church performs much the same function. Legend has it that Peel's loathing of village gossip – especially about himself – led to some houses being built with 'front' doors at the back, though quite how he expected this to eliminate the problem is not clear.

A version of the Way, at present unofficial, bears right at the green, following Heathley Lane (not a right of way as yet) to Heathley Farm **B**, then joining a right of way to Hill Farm and on to the A453 where you turn left for about 60 yards, then right over a stile and follow a path to Hints Farm. When this version of the route becomes official it will be the preferred option. Until that time, follow the road past the Post Office/General Store and the church and turn sharp right with it, following it to the main road.

Turn left and follow the road for 330 yards (300m), then go right along Bangley Lane (not named but signed as a 'Private Estate Road'. Walk up the lane, with a marvellous view

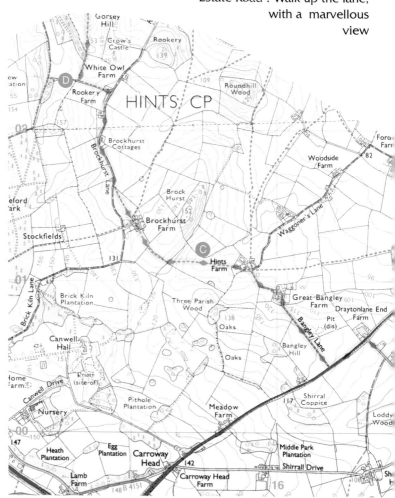

to the right over the Midland Plain. Follow the lane to the right, passing Bangley Farm and Bangley View (with delightful pigs on the gateposts), then bear left with the lane past a fine new building and continue to Hints Farm. There, bear left along a muddy track, passing the farmhouse on the right and following a tractor track (with a single strand wire fence on right) past an oak tree and go on to a gap between three oaks on the left and a telegraph pole on the right **C**. Now go uphill to the top left-hand field corner. Cross a stile and the field ahead, picking up an old hedge line, then aim to the right of the house (Brockhurst Farm) ahead. Exit the field, cross a building site, with the farmhouse on the left, and go over a stile. Maintain direction to cut off the corner of the field beyond, crossing a stile in the far hedge on to a lane. Turn right, following the lane past Brockhurst Cottages (on the right, No. 95 is looking a bit forlorn and begging the question of where the other 94 cottages are situated) and the superb Brockhurst Park Farm on the left. Now turn left through Rookery Farm. Go through a gate and along a track and then, before the next gate **D,** go over a stile on the right, beside a gate, and follow the hedge on the left to a stile.

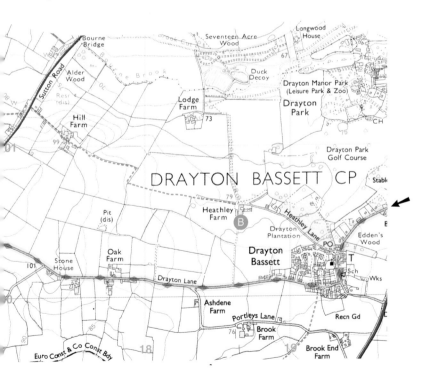

Go over the rise ahead and maintain direction down a marvellous valley with a view towards Lichfield. Cross a stile/gate and continue to reach a stile in the top right-hand corner of a field. Bear right to follow the edge of the crop, on the left, following the field edge around to the left and crossing a stile on the right. Follow a fence and then a hedge on the right, crossing a stile by a gate and, soon, a footbridge. Now follow the drive of the house on the left, bearing right at a fork to reach the A5.

The village of Weeford **67** lies to the left, just off the main road. It has a good restaurant, The Old Schoolhouse, opposite the early nineteenth-century St Mary's Church. The church has late sixteenth-century Dutch stained glass windows brought from the chapel of the Dukes of Orleans in Paris in 1803 – a very strange provenance. The

Beyond Rookery Farm, the Way descends a lovely valley to reach Buck's Head Farm on the outskirts of the village of Weeford.

village was the birthplace of James Wyatt, a distant relative of Lichfield's Dr Samuel Johnson and a mechanical genius who, in 1738, patented the first mechanical spinning machine with rollers that were turned by donkeys. Wyatt set up a cotton mill in Birmingham, but Richard Arkwright's spinning jenny was a better machine and replaced the donkey-driven spinner.

Cross the road with care and turn right to reach Buck's Head Farm **E** on the left. Follow the lane through the farmyard, then climb gently, with a hedge on your right. Where the track goes right to Buck's Head Cottages, continue straight ahead along the edge of a field with a hedge on your right. Go through a hedge gap at the field corner to rejoin the track and turn left down it. Follow the track to a gate on to a crossing track. Go right for 20 yards, then left over a bridleway and follow the track ahead.

Dr Johnson gloomily contemplates the stalls in Market Square, Lichfield.

Go straight over at a crossing track and continue to reach a road **F**. Go straight across, following a wide gravel track past an entrance to Packington Moor Farm's 'Pick Your Own' on the left. Continue ahead along a narrow, hedged track to reach a metal gate. Maintain direction, soon with a hedge on the right. The track bears left to Horsley Brook Farm: go through the metal gate ahead and cross a small field to reach another metal gate. Maintain direction along the track ahead with a hedge on the right, going through a wooden gate and across a field to reach a stile/wooden gate on to a track, with Ingley Hill Farm on the left. Go through a metal gate and follow the fence on the left to reach a track that goes to Freeford Home Farm on the right and a house on the left. Maintain direction downhill to cross a private drive. Cross a stile and follow the hedge on the left to reach a gate. Follow the track ahead, with a house on the right and a rabbit warren, with resident stoat, on the left to reach the main road.

Turn left along the main road, passing the Horse and Jockey Inn **68** on the right. Cross the bridge over the A38 and continue for a further 660 yards (600m), ignoring Ryknild Street on the right. Take the next turning to the right, Quarry Hills Lane **G**, there is a Heart of

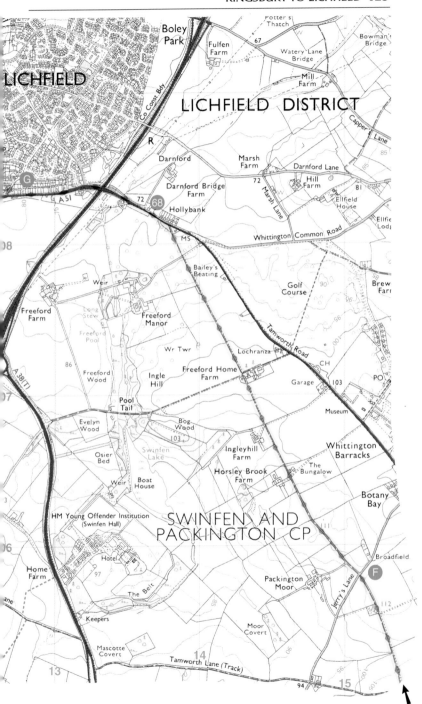

England Way brass plaque set in the pavement here. Turn first left along Borrowcop Lane, and then first right up Hillside. Bear left and then right, ignore the path on the left (opposite Minor's Hill) continuing around a right-hand bend. Turn left along a metalled path between Nos 45 and 47, continuing across open land and then beside a wall on the right. Ignore a path on the left and you will reach a road (take the left branch of the two-path 'prongs' ahead) by guard rails. Cross, to a further set of rails, following a metalled, then a paved, path to a road (Oakhurst). Turn left, bearing right with the road to reach a T-junction (with Cherry Orchard). Cross, bearing slightly to the right, and follow the path beyond the 'No-Cycling' sign. The spires of Lichfield cathedral can now be seen ahead and there is another brass Heart of England Way plaque set in the pavement. Follow the path (Frenchman's Walk) across a footbridge over the railway to reach a road opposite the Christadelphian Hall. Turn left, bearing right with the road 'No Through Road – Levetts Fields' to reach a T-junction. Cross at the pedestrian lights and go through the arch of the Three Spires Shopping Centre. Turn left, then bear right to reach Bore Street. On your way you will pass a square to your left: in it stands the Guildhall, a fourteenth-century building which has been the city court, the prison and a theatre. It now houses the City Dungeons, with the old stocks and other items housed in the original cells. Lichfield is, perhaps, a fitting place for such a grim museum as it was the last place in England where a 'heretic' was burnt at the stake. The unfortunate man concerned was Edward Weightman who faced the flames in 1612.

Step right beside a lovely building, now occupied by Boots the Chemist, then continue along Conduit Street, passing Market Square (with St Mary's Church and the statues of Dr Samuel Johnson and Boswell to the left). Maintain direction along Dam Street passing the Garrick Coffee House (the best in the town) and Causeway House on the right. Go past Minster Pool on the left to reach a T-junction. Turn left, passing the cathedral **69** and Cathedral Close on the right, to reach a T-junction. The ugly house at the eastern end of the Close is said to have been built by an unpleasant woman determined to ruin her sister's view of Stowe Pond, a picturesque expanse of water which lies to the east of the cathedral. Turn right along Beacon Street, passing Erasmus Darwin's house on the corner. Darwin was born near Newark in 1731, studied medicine at Cambridge and Edinburgh and lived in Lichfield from 1756-81. He was a very able and popular physician, a poet and a botanist whose books on the topic were a significant contribution to the subject. Erasmus was the grandfather of Charles Darwin and in some of his writings actually anticipated the theories of his more illustrious grandson. Erasmus Darwin moved to Derby in 1781 and died there in 1802.

Turn first left along Shaw Lane, bearing right through a car park at the bottom. Follow the walled path ahead, then continue through Beacon Park to reach another car park. In Beacon Park there is a statue of Commander Edward John Smith, the captain of the *Titanic*. Smith was actually born in Hanley, Stoke-on-Trent, the statue being erected here as his birthplace lies within the see of Lichfield. Go through the car park, then continue around a golf course on the left. Maintain direction along the path ahead to reach the A51.

7 LICHFIELD TO MILFORD

via Cannock Chase 15 miles (24 km)

Cross the A51 with care and go over a stile into a field **A**. Go diagonally across the field towards the trees in the corner and cross a stile on to Pipe Green Trust land. Bear right, with a hedge on the right, until a wooden fence comes into view. Head towards this, bearing right before reaching it to go over a stile. Now follow a track parallel to a drive to reach a road at the entrance to the drive leading to Maple Hayes Hall Dyslexia School and Research Centre. Turn left and follow the road. Be careful: the road is narrow (sometimes very narrow where it has been carved through the sandstone) and twisting, with no verges and few escape places. Go past Abnalls Cottage and Green End on the right, then turn right over a stile and go diagonally across a field. Maintain direction to reach a stile which is, at first, out of sight below the 'edge' of the field. Follow the hedge on the left to a stile, then aim to the left of Keeper's Lodge **70** on the horizon, crossing three stiles, the last of which is to the left as you reach the garden fence, on to a road.

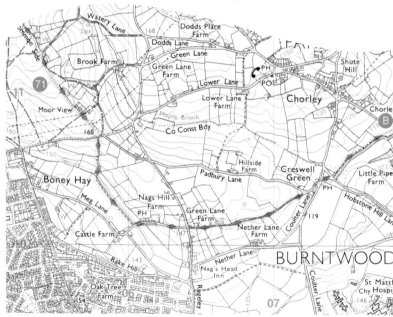

Turn right, bearing right at a junction to pass Brook Cottages and reach a stream just before the village sign for Chorley **B**. Turn left over a stile beside a metal gate and walk with the stream on your left, crossing fields linked by stiles to reach a stile (the third) into a small wood. Follow the path through the wood and cross a footbridge to reach a lane at a junction. Go straight ahead, soon reaching a T-junction where you turn left, then right by the Nelson Inn (along a road signed for Boney Hay). Now turn left along a track (not sharp left along a drive) following it for about half a mile (1km), passing a very attractive lake on the right near the end. The track reaches a road at a T-junction: go straight over and along Springle Stych Lane to reach the Drill Inn. Continue along the road, crossing a stream, and then turning right over a stile beside a gate. Follow the fence/hedge and stream on the right to reach a stiled footbridge, on the right, just before the field end. Climb to a stile and continue with a hedge on your right, crossing two stiles, the second on to a road at Gentleshaw Common **71**. Go right for about 20 yards then turn left along a road signed for Gentleshaw and Beaudesert. Walk beside the road (soon going under power lines) across Gentleshaw Common. The Common is an SSSI consisting of over 200 acres of heathland, chiefly heather, gorse and bilberry, which forms a rare wildlife habitat. With sheep no longer grazing the Common, bracken has invaded and to preserve the old landscape this is cut down.

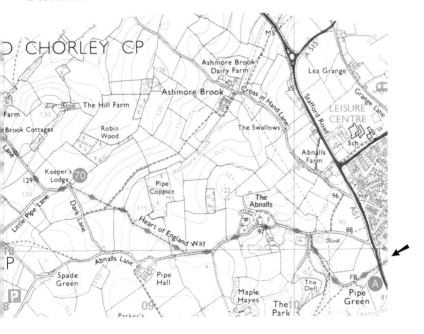

The heather is also cut periodically to promote new growth, this also helps the wildlife. Skylarks, now declining in numbers due to changes in farming practices, are still found here, though the wayfarer's best find would not be a bird, but a glimpse of the green hairstreak butterfly, one of Britain's rarest, which still thrives on Gentleshaw.

As you cross the Common, look back along the Way: on clear days the spires of Lichfield Cathedral – the Ladies of the Vale – can be seen from here. Go past the Windmill Inn, and the old windmill **72** that supplies the name, then a church and school on the right to reach a turning on the left. Step left, then go ahead through a kissing gate beside the gate for the Chestall Estate **C**. Walk along a fine avenue to join a tarmac drive coming from the right. Continue beside the metal railings of the reservoir on the left, and where these go sharp left, go with them **D** walking between the railings and a wood on the right to reach a kissing gate on to a road at a junction, with the Beaudesert Scout and Guide Camp Activity Centre to the right. Go straight ahead along the road, then turn right into the car park for the Castle Ring hill fort **73**. Hill forts were used by Iron Age (Celtic) farming communities as safe refuges in the event of attack by marauding 'pirates' or other tribes. The 9-acre Castle Ring site is protected by a series of ditches and ramparts, at least two sets on all sides, and four sets on the eastern side where the natural slope is gentlest. Early forts used only a single ditch and rampart, but the invention of the sling shot meant that wider defences were needed to keep the besiegers at bay. Castle Ring is therefore a later hill fort, or was modified after its first construction, dating probably to the last centuries BC. In its original form it would have had a wooden stockade wall on top of the inner rampart and a heavily fortified gate protecting the entrance through the defences. Excavations inside the fort suggest that it was occupied (perhaps not continuously) until 500AD. There may even have been a hunting lodge here in medieval times.

Go past the barrier at the end of the car park. The hill fort is reached by way of the wooden staircase ahead, but the Way bears left along a track leading through the woodland of Beaudesert, once the heart of the Bishop's Chase but now Cannock's eastern edge, to reach a T-junction with a crossing track. Turn left for 10 yards, then turn right, downhill, soon bearing right along a wider track. Go straight ahead at a crosstracks, then bear left along the narrower track at a track fork. Ford two small streams, the second flowing from a beautiful pond on the left which, on my last visit, was home to a family of tufted ducks. Now maintain direction over a crossing track to reach a point 5 yards from a road **E**. Here, turn right along a narrow path, following it to a broad track. Turn left along the track to reach the road. Turn right, then left

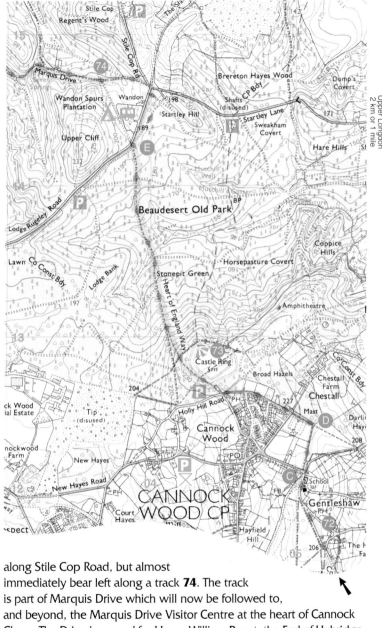

along Stile Cop Road, but almost
immediately bear left along a track **74**. The track
is part of Marquis Drive which will now be followed to,
and beyond, the Marquis Drive Visitor Centre at the heart of Cannock
Chase. The Drive is named for Henry William Paget, the Earl of Uxbridge
and Beaudesert, who was also Marquis of Anglesey. The Marquis was
cavalry commander and second-in-command to the Duke of Wellington

After welcoming wayfarers to Lichfield, the cathedral's spires mark the last view of the city as the Way heads west towards Cannock Chase.

at Waterloo and is famous for the exchange between himself and the Duke after a cannonball had taken the Marquis' leg off as the pair were watching the progress of the battle from horseback. Most versions of the conversation have the Marquis saying 'My God, I've lost my leg' and the Duke responding with 'My God, so you have'. But I prefer the more surreal suggestion that the exchange was 'My God, there goes me leg.' 'My God so it does.' The Marquis seems to have been loved and respected by the folk of his estates. On Anglesey a statue of him, astride a column and with both legs, greets visitors arriving over the Britannia Bridge, while here in the Midlands, 10,000 tenants are said to have greeted him on his return from Waterloo, hauling his carriage by hand from Lichfield to Beaudesert. Perhaps the adulation stemmed from the idea that he was a man's man: he had eight children in nine years by his first wife, Lady Caroline Villiers, and when she died (from exhaustion ?) he had ten more by Lady Charlotte Wellesley.

Follow the track to a gate by a house, on the right. Go through or around the gate, then pass another fine pond on the left. Where a track joins from the left: continue ahead to reach a metalled track from the Moors Gorse Pumping Station, on the left. The Station preserves a steam-powered Cornish beam engine designed by James Watt's company and still capable of raising over two million gallons of water every day. Cross the track to reach the main road (the A460). Cross the road and the railway ahead with extreme care and continue along the track beyond. The woodland to the left is Furnace Coppice, named for an iron smelter constructed here so as to be close to the coppiced trees which supplied its charcoal fuel. The track climbs Kitbag Hill **75,** so-called because aircraftmen arriving at the station at the base of the hill during the 1939-45 War had to carry their kitbags up to the camp at the top. Ignore tracks joining from the right to reach a metalled lane at a huge waymarker post for the Cross Chase Walk. Continue along the lane, soon passing paths on the left to the Cannock Chase Visitor Centre **76** which stands in a clearing occupied by RAF Hednesford during the 1939-45 War. The Centre has information on the Chase and the various walking and cycling routes through it. There are toilets and a picnic site, but no refreshments.

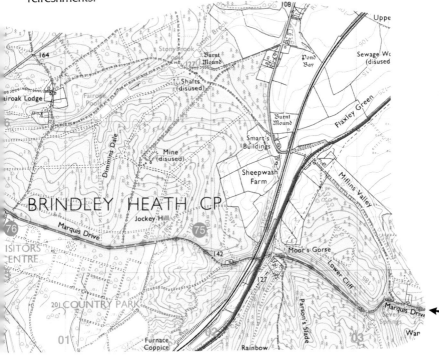

Continue along the metalled track, going through a gate by the Burma Star Memorial Copse on the left, and following the track to reach a road. Bear right to reach a cross roads at Flints Corner. Turn right and immediately left (or cut the corner by going straight across) and follow a track through woodland. Go right, then left at a crossing track, then right and left again at the next crossing track. Now continue to reach a road **F**. Cross and follow a track downhill, with woodland to the right, to reach a track junction. Turn left, now with woodland on both sides, continuing downhill and crossing Sher Brook to reach a cross-tracks. Go straight ahead, climbing, with woodland (chiefly Corsican pine, but with some Scots pine) closing in on both sides. Go over a rise and descend, passing the Katyn Memorial **77** on the right, to reach a road. The stone commemorates the murder of 14,000 Polish army officers and intellectuals in the Katyn Forest in 1940. The mass grave of the victims, all killed by a bullet in the back of the neck, was discovered by the Germans in 1943. With the 1939-45 War still in progress and the Soviet Union on the Allied side, it was then, and later, claimed that the Germans had perpetrated the atrocity, but it is now known that Stalin ordered the killings to deprive Poland of leadership as a prelude to a Soviet takeover.

Turn right, going uphill into woodland and follow the track through the trees and across the heathland of Anson's Bank to reach a road and

The lucky visitor to Cannock Chase may catch sight of a fallow deer.

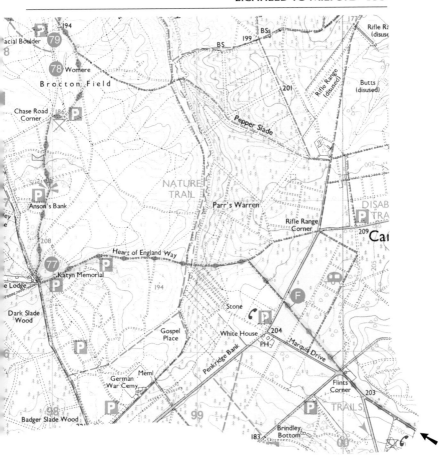

car park. The name comes from the
Anson family of Shugborough. Admiral George Anson sailed around
the world in his ship *Centurion* in 1740. To commemorate the feat his
brother Thomas planted groups of Scots pine in prominent positions
on the heathland from here to Milford. There is a toposcope on the
Bank pointing out the highlights of an excellent view. On clear days
the Wrekin in Shropshire can be seen.

In the car park, bear left, uphill, to reach open heathland. Turn left at
a cross-tracks, heading towards the woodland in the distance. To the
left is Womere **78,** an upland marsh pool, one of very few in central
England. Folklore has it that the pool is bottomless, though in reality
such pools are actually very shallow. Now climb to reach a waymarker
post on the right and a trig point on the left. A short distance from the
trig point is the Glacial Boulder **79,** a glacial 'erratic'. Glaciers gouge out

The paths on Cannock Chase run wide and clear through beautiful heathland, but caution is needed as the area is criss-crossed with tracks.

the rock over which they travel, grinding most of it to a fine paste which is deposited as glacial moraine at the limit of the glacier's travel. Occasionally a boulder will be carried within the ice rather than being ground beneath it and will be deposited when the ice retreats. Such 'erratics', so-called because they did not correspond to the local geology, were a puzzle to early geologists. It was not until the Ice Ages and the movements of glaciers were understood that the mechanism which deposited such boulders was recognized. This particular erratic was brought to Cannock Chase from south-west Scotland.

The Staffordshire Way joins the Heart of England Way from the left at the trig point: but our route maintains direction, going downhill and ignoring the Staffordshire Way as it turns right **G**. Go steeply downhill, crossing a semi-metalled track and then continue downhill before climbing to reach a waymarker post and a crossing track. Turn left, crossing a large track and heading down the Mere Valley. The track bears right, then left to reach a waymarker and signpost with the information that you are only 3/4 mile (1.2km) from Milford. Ignore the track going right and continue downhill, bearing right at the next waymarker before going uphill slightly and then descending to reach another waymarker. Bear right along a track joining from the left, passing the Sister Dora Home for the Elderly on the left. Continue downhill to reach the car park on Milford Common **80**. In the village beyond there is an inn and a couple of cafés. One of these is a Wimpey bar, so you can, if you are so inclined, claim that your walk finished, not with a bang but a Wimpey!

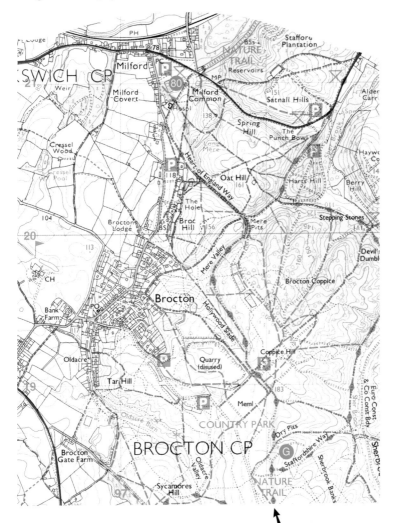

USEFUL
INFORMATION

Transport

There are railway stations at Cheltenham and Moreton-in-Marsh, buses from both run to Bourton-on-the-Water. Bourton is also connected by bus to other Cotswold towns and, through them, to Gloucester and Oxford, both of which are also on mainline railway routes. Further information on Gloucestershire bus services can be obtained from:
Gloucestershire County Council, Shire Hall, Gloucester GL1 2TG. Tel. 01242 425543

There is a railway station at Stafford from where it is possible to get a bus to Milford. As it is only 5 miles (8 km) from the station to Milford by way of a footpath beside the River Sow, and then the towpath of the Staffordshire and Worcestershire Canal, many walkers prefer to use Stafford as the starting or finishing point of their walk.
Information on bus services in Staffordshire can be obtained from:
Staffordshire County Council, Highways House, Riverway, Stafford ST16 3TJ. Tel. 01785 223344

For those wishing to start at intermediate points, there are train stations at Henley-in-Arden and Lichfield. Information on bus services in Warwickshire can be obtained from:
Warwickshire County Council, PT and ES, Barrack Street, Warwick CV34 4SX. Tel. 01926 410410

Accomodation

Accommodation is available at most of the towns and villages along the Way, and at all the places at which this Guide's chapters start and end. Tourist Information Offices also have lists of accommodation. An up-to-date list of accommodation, including bed-and-breakfast sites and camp sites can also be obtained by sending a stamped addressed envelope to:
Heart of England List, 8 Hillside Close, Bartley Green, Birmingham B32 4LT.

There are no Youth Hostels along the Way.

TOURIST INFORMATION OFFICES

The whole of the Way lies within the area of the Heart of England Tourist Board whose main office is at:
Heart of England Tourist Board, Larkhill Road, Worcester WR5 2EZ. Tel. 01905 763436

There are Tourist Information Offices at the following places:
Chipping Campden, The Town Hall, Chipping Campden GL55 6AT.
  Tel. 01386 841206 (open in summer only)
Lichfield, Donegal House, Bore Street, Lichfield WS13 6NE.
  Tel. 01543 252109
Stafford, Ancient High House, Greengate Street, Stafford ST16 2HS.
  Tel. 01785 240204
Stow-on-the-Wold, Hollis House, The Square, Stow-on-the-Wold,
  GL54 1AF. Tel. 01451 831082
Stratford-upon-Avon, Bridgefoot, Stratford-upon-Avon CV37 6GW.
  Tel. 01789 293127
Warwick, The Court Hose, Jury Street, Warwick CV34 4EW.
  Tel. 01926 492212

USEFUL ADDRESSES

British Trust for Ornithology, Beech Grove, Tring, Herts HP12 5NR.
The Countryside Commission, John Dower House, Crescent Place,
  Cheltenham, GL50 3RA. Tel. 01242 521381
English Heritage (Midlands Region), Hazelrigg House, 33 Marefair,
  Northampton NN1 1SR. Tel. 01604 730320
English Heritage (South-West Region), 7-8 King Street, Bristol BS1
  4EQ. Tel. 0117 9750700
The National Trust (Head Office), 36 Queen Anne's Gate, London
  SW1H 9AS. Tel. 0171 222 9251
The National Trust (Severn Region), Mythe End House,
  Tewkesbury, Glos GL20 6EB. Tel. 01684 850051
The National Trust (East Midlands Region), Clumber Park
  Stableyard, Worksop S80 3BE. Tel. 01909 486411
Ordnance Survey, Romsey Road, Maybush, Southampton
  SO16 4GU.
The Ramblers' Association, 1-5 Wandsworth Road, London SW8
  2XX. Tel. 0171 582 6878
The Royal Society for Nature Conservation, The Green,
  Witham Park, Waterside South, Lincoln LN5 7JR.
  Tel. 01522 544400

The Royal Society for the Protection of Birds (RSPB), The Lodge, Sandy, Beds SG19 2DL. Tel. 01767 680551

Wildlife Trusts:

Gloucestershire: Gloucestershire Trust for Nature Conservation, Dulverton Building, Robinswood Hill Country Park, Reservoir Road, Gloucester GL4 9SX. Tel. 01452 383333

Staffordshire: Staffordshire Wildlife Trust, Coutts House, Sandon, Stafford ST18 0DN. Tel. 01889 508534/508442

Warwickshire: Warwickshire Wildlife Trust, Brandon Marsh Nature Centre, Brandon Lane, Coventry CV3 3GW. Tel. 01203 302912

ORDNANCE SURVEY MAPS COVERING THE HEART OF ENGLAND WAY

Landranger Maps (scale 1:50 000)

150 Worcester and the Malverns

151 Stratford-upon-Avon

128 Derby and Burton upon Trent

139 Birmingham

140 Leicester, Coventry and Rugby

127 Stafford

163 Cheltenham and Cirencester area

Pathfinder Maps (scale 1:25 000)

1067 Winchcombe and Stow-on-the-Wold*

1043 Broadway and Chipping Campden*

1020 Vale of Evesham

997 Stratford-upon-Avon (West) and Alcester

975 Redditch and Henley-in-Arden

976 Warwick and Royal Leamington Spa

955 Coventry (South) and Kenilworth

935 Coventry (North) and Meriden

914 Nuneaton

913 Sutton Coldfield and Walsall

893 Tamworth

892 Lichfield and Brownhills

* These two pathfinders are to be withdrawn in Spring 1998 when they will be replaced with a new Outdoor Leisure Map, 45 The Cotswolds.

Explorer Map (1: 25,000)

6 Cannock Chase and Chasewater

BIBLIOGRAPHY

Belcher, Sherry and Mills, Mary (compilers), Cannock Chase, Alan Sutton.

Bird, Vivian, *A Short History of Warwickshire and Birmingham*, Batsford 1977.

Warwickshire, Batsford, 1973.

Boswell, James, *The Life of Johnson*, OUP World Classics.

Boughey, Joseph, *Hadfield's British Canals*, Alan Sutton, 1994.

Ditchfield, P H, *Memorials of Old Gloucestershire*, George Allen, 1911.

Hadfield, Charles, *British Canals*, David and Charles, 1984.

Hidman, Douglas, *Warwickshire*, Faber and Faber, 1979.

Musson, A E, *The Growth of British Industry*, Batsford, 1978.

Nelson J P, *Chipping Campden - Some Aspects of the Past and Present of a North*

Cotswold Country Town and its surrounding District, published by the author, 1975.

Pevsner, Nikolaus, *The Buildings of England: Staffordshire*, Penguin.

Pevsner, Nikolaus and Wedgwood, Alexandra, *The Buildings of England: Warwickshire*, Penguin.

Saville, G (Alcester and District Local History Society), *Alcester: A History*, KAF Brewin Books, Studley.

The Victorian History of Staffordshire: Volume 14, OUP.

Verey, David, *The Buildings of England: Gloucestershire and the Cotswolds*, Penguin.

PLACES TO VISIT ON OR NEAR THE HEART OF ENGLAND WAY

Bourton-on-the-Water
Birdland, Cotswold Motor Museum and Toy Collection, Dragonfly Maze, Folly Farm Waterfowl, Model Railway Exhibition, Model Village, Perfumery Exhibition, Village Life Exhibition.

Lower Slaughter
The Old Mill Museum.

Bourton on the Hill
Batsford Park Arboretum, Cotswold Falconry Centre, Sezincote House and Gardens.

Blockley
Sleepy Hollow Farm Park.

Chipping Campden
Ernest Wilson Memorial Garden, St John's Church, Silk Mill Handicrafts Centre.

Mickleton
Hidcote Manor Garden (NT), Kiftsgate Court Gardens.

Honeybourne (near Bidford)
Domestic Fowl Trust.

Wixford
Antique Doll Collection.

Alcester
Coughton Court (NT), Kinwarton Dovecote, Ragley Hall, Tthe Shakespeare properties at, or near, Stratford-upon-Avon lie just to the east.
Henley-in-Arden
Guildhall.
Baddesley Clinton
Baddesley Clinton Manor (NT), Packwood House,
Oldwick Lane
Oldwych Gallery, Oldwych House Farm.
Kenilworth
Abbey Fields, Kenilworth Castle.
Berkswell
Berkswell Museum, Berkswell Windmill.
Meriden
National Motorcycle Museum.
Kingsbury
Broomey Croft Rare Breeds Farm, Kingsbury Water Park

Visitor Centre, Middleton Hall and Craft Centre.
Drayton Bassett
Drayton Manor Family Theme Park and Zoo.
Tamworth
Tamworth Castle, Tamworth Snowdome.
Lichfield
Guildhall/City Dungeon, Heart of the Country Craft Centre,Lichfield Cathedral, Lichfield Heritage Exhibition and Treasury, Museum of the Staffordshire Regiment, Samuel Johnson Birthplace Museum, Wall (Letocetum) Roman Site.
Cannock Chase
Visitor Centres, Valley Heritage Centre/Cannock Chase Museum.
Milford
Midland Crafts, Wolsley Bridge, Shugborough Hall (NT).